Spiritual Excellence

Richard B. Eason

Spiritual Excellence
The Path to Happiness, Holiness, and Heaven

EWTN PUBLISHING, INC.
Irondale, Alabama

EWTN Publishing, Inc.
5817 Old Leeds Road, Irondale, AL 35210

Distributed by Sophia Institute Press, Box 5284, Manchester, NH 03108.

paperback ISBN 978-1-68278-277-4

ebook ISBN 978-1-68278-278-1

Library of Congress Control Number: 2021951371

First printing

For Rosalyn, Blake, Kyle, Grant, Ashley, Evan, and Clare

Spiritual excellence is contagious!
CATCH IT!

Contents

Part III
Remedies to Restore Our Souls to a
Natural State of Happiness and Holiness
and Lead Us to Heaven

Part IV
An Individual Spiritual Plan of Excellence
That Leads to a Life of Happiness,
Holiness, and Heaven

Part V
The Saints as Role Models
of Spiritual Excellence

Daily Oath to Jesus to Pursue Holiness and Spiritual Excellence

I will practice strict spiritual self-discipline with a complete surrender of my will to You;

I will pray throughout the day and always listen to Your voice, never letting my heart go astray to work for the evil one and preventing any sinful, selfish temptation from entering my soul;

I will trust in You for everything in my life and be obedient to You, allowing my thoughts, words, and actions to come from You and never from myself;

I will act like one of Your saints, practicing holiness and spiritual excellence with great spiritual integrity and spiritual enthusiasm;

I will conduct a daily examination of my soul with You as to whether I lived up to this oath to pursue holiness and spiritual excellence, and I will seek forgiveness and mercy from You for any sinfulness.

Preface

Many people in America today are struggling with all kinds of issues in their families, jobs, health, and future. Happiness and holiness are often missing and have been replaced by stress, anxiety, and worry. We are searching for a remedy but have not been able to find one. The simple answer to these questions is to learn to pursue spiritual excellence, doing the will of Jesus as a way of life. Spiritual excellence is the path to happiness, holiness, and Heaven.

This book contains the proof that the daily pursuit of spiritual excellence is the way back to the abundant life that Our Lord is calling us to experience. The book is based on inspirations from the Holy Spirit, over 160 Scripture quotations, teachings from more than twenty saints and numerous spiritual authors, and the *Catechism of the Catholic Church*.

The book begins with how to get started on the path to spiritual excellence. It continues with answers to these questions: Why am I the way that I am, and how did I get to this point in my life? Next, the reader is asked to do a spiritual self-audit to identify the specific issues that negatively impact him or her, which is followed by an analysis of these challenges. Then we explore the remedies for these issues. Lastly, the reader develops

Spiritual Excellence

an Individual Spiritual Plan (ISP) for overcoming these challenges: a permanent resolution leading to a life dedicated to spiritual excellence and the path to happiness, holiness, and Heaven—always doing the will of Jesus.

Each chapter is only a few pages long and focuses in on the heart of each topic. The chapter begins with a story that sets up the topic, followed by a discussion which includes references to Scripture and teachings of the saints and spiritual authors. The chapter concludes with a couple of spiritual treasures for reflection and space for individual spiritual thoughts.

You are at the dawn of an opportunity to fly with the angels and soar with the saints to a happier and holier life. Get on the path to spiritual excellence that will make your life 1,000 percent better and lead you to Heaven.

Acknowledgments

Putting this book together has never been an act of labor. It has always been a joyful journey guided exclusively by the Holy Spirit. Every word in this book comes from Him. The time spent writing this book on spiritual excellence will be well spent if by the grace of the Holy Spirit, a soul reading it will become closer to Jesus, thereby getting on the path to happiness, holiness, and Heaven.

Thanks so much to all the people who helped to shape my life and helped me to truly understand the meaning of spiritual excellence. Thanks to my mother, Mary Eason, and my father, Rudy Eason, for their endless efforts in raising me in the practice of the Catholic faith. Thanks to my wife, Rosalyn, for being a true holy soul, for her many hours editing and improving this work, and for bringing our three boys into the world. Thanks to our three sons and daughter-in-law, who are Blake, Kyle, Grant, and Ashley, for their continued dedication to the Catholic faith.

The original audience for this book was my three sons and my daughter-in-law. The goal was to pass along a spiritual legacy to them that would help them build a stronger relationship with Jesus and get to Heaven. Many thanks to Msgr. Christopher Nalty of Good Shepard Parish and Fr. Joe Kraft of Notre Dame Seminary for their initial review of this book and their encouragement to

Spiritual Excellence

spread the concept of spiritual excellence to others. Thanks to
Raymond Arroyo for all his help and guidance in pursuing the
publication of this book, and to Gwyn Cassou for formatting and
typing many drafts of it. My gratitude to Daniel Hopkins and
Anna Maria Dube for their editing work and to Devin Jones of
EWTN and Nora Malone for their efforts in getting this book
in final form for publication.

Spiritual Excellence

Part I

Introduction

Getting Started on the Path
to Spiritual Excellence

Over 7,500,000,000 people live on the earth. We are all on a journey with one goal in mind: to get to Heaven. Many of us are missing something in our lives and can't quite figure out what it is. We are worried and sometimes anxious about our families, jobs, health, and future. There are many questions but so few answers.

Why am I the way that I am?

How did I get to this point in my life?

Why do I seem to get emotionally bounced around all the time by my work, friends, or family?

What is God calling me to do with my life?

Why am I robbed of happiness and holiness by issues such as questionable faith, temptation, suffering, stress, worry, fear, conflict, laziness, greed, anger, self-pride, and selfishness?

What remedies are available to change my life and restore my happiness and holiness, such as learning to pursue spiritual excellence, putting the power of the Holy Spirit to work, identifying what God is calling me to do, evolving into a rock for Jesus, restoring our families to holiness, receiving forgiveness of my sins, feeding my soul by the Holy Eucharist, finding true lasting peace, developing a rich prayer life, making good decisions, spreading the good news, and working with my guardian angel? And is Heaven a real place?

Is there an individualized plan of excellence to follow that will provide a permanent solution from Jesus for the issues that I face?

The chapters to come answer all these questions and provide a path to spiritual excellence that leads us to happiness, holiness, and Heaven. The first step is to consider why I am the way that I am and how I got to this point in my life (part I). The second step is to do a spiritual self-audit (SSA) to identify the issues that negatively affect us and to know how to analyze them (part II). The third step is to provide remedies for these issues which will make our lives 1,000 percent better (part III). The last step is to develop and follow an individualized spiritual plan (ISP) from God that will be a permanent resolution for these negative issues and that will result in a life dedicated to spiritual excellence (part IV). The final part of the book refers to several saints who are wonderful role models of spiritual excellence (part V).

For some people, tweaking is all that is needed to achieve spiritual excellence. But for others, a more in-depth consideration of the issues and remedies may be required. At this point in time, all of us are on the spectrum of spiritual excellence.

On the front end of the spectrum, there are those who lack a relationship with Jesus and who have little faith. On the other end, there are those who have their soul on autopilot, always guided by our Lord. At the end of the day, we all want to be on the right side of the spectrum, walking with our Lord and Savior and in constant pursuit of spiritual excellence. This will give us a continuous state of happiness and holiness in seeking our eternal reward of Heaven with Jesus.

There are statistics that show only 57 percent of people who begin reading a book will finish it. Please don't be in the 43 percent that doesn't finish because you will miss out on an opportunity that will change your life forever.

All of this material in this book is based on over 160 Bible quotations and references as well as teachings from more than twenty saints, including St. Paul, St. Teresa of Ávila, St. Ignatius of Loyola, St. Thérèse of Lisieux, St. Maria Faustina Kowalska, and Pope St. John Paul II, other spiritual writers, and the *Catechism of the Catholic Church*. Moreover, the Holy Spirit guided and inspired me in writing this book. At all times, I have been under the mantel of our Blessed Mother Mary. This book is a true oasis for a troubled world.

In the Bible, St. Paul tells us, "Do not conform yourself to this age but be transformed by the renewal of your mind, that you may discern what is the will of God, what is good and pleasing and perfect" (Rom. 12:2). He further tells us to think about spiritual excellence when he says, "Now as you excel in every respect, in faith, discourse, knowledge, all earnestness, and in the love we have for you, may you excel in this gracious act (generosity) also" (2 Cor. 8:7). Also, he wants us to pursue spiritual excellence when he says, "Finally, brothers, whatever is true, whatever is honorable, whatever is just, whatever is pure, whatever is lovely, whatever is gracious, if there is any excellence and if there is anything worthy of praise, think about these things." (Phil. 4:8).

The most effective way to read this book is slowly, one chapter a day. Each chapter is only a few pages, taking just minutes to read. After reading the chapter, spend some time thinking about it. At the end of each chapter is a list of Scripture passages or key phrases from spiritual writers from the chapter to aid your reflection. Consider writing one or two thoughts from your reflections in the space provided at the end of each chapter.

Spiritual Excellence

Within a few days of reading a couple of chapters, your heart and soul will feel a huge uptick on your happiness meter. This change is a function of the Holy Spirit working in your life. As you continue to read this book, your life will be transformed by our Lord's graces working in your heart. The pursuit of spiritual excellence, by doing the will of God, will become a way of life that will lead to Heaven.

When you are finished reading this book, pass it on to others so they can obtain a life of happiness and peace. One of our missions from Jesus is to bring others closer to Him by our efforts. St. Teresa of Ávila said it best: "Christ has no body now but yours. No hands, no feet on earth but yours. Yours are the eyes through which He looks compassion on this world. Yours are the feet with which He walks to do good. Yours are the hands through which He blesses all the world. Yours are the hands, yours are the feet, yours are the eyes, you are His body. Christ has no body now on earth but yours."[1]

---

[1] *The Collected Works of St. Teresa of Ávila* (Washington, DC: ICS Publications, 2012).

Why Am I the Person That I Am?
How Did I Get to This Point in My Life?

To answer these questions, we have to consider our physical, psychological, and spiritual makeup. Our physical being is often the easiest to understand. Height, eye color, facial structure, and intelligence are a function of genetics from our parents. We have no choice regarding these physical attributes. On the contrary, our psychological makeup and spiritual being are often a matter of individual choice, influenced by our family of origin, the role models we have chosen, and the people we associate with.

What do we mean when we say family of origin? This concept refers to our upbringing by parents and close family members such as grandparents, siblings, aunts, and uncles. Another way to say this is that each one of us is a product of the way we were raised. If the home life we grew up in was filled with Christian values, quality family time, and a good learning environment, then our family of origin was most likely a positive experience for us. By contrast, if the atmosphere at home was filled with substance abuse, physical abuse, emotional abuse, and/or constant adversity and conflict, then our family of origin may have left us with psychological and emotional scars.

Spiritual Excellence

Role models such as educators, coaches, priests, religious, neighbors, and extended family members have also made an impact on us. If someone asked you to name your best teacher and why, the answer would likely be the teacher who stimulated you to learn and grow intellectually. To the contrary, a teacher who humiliated or ignored you in the classroom was probably a harmful influence. A favorite uncle or coach or on the other hand, an abusive family member, or community leader, can also produce this same type of positive or negative impact.

There are still others who have made an impact on us. It is often said that we become like those we associate with. There are friends and acquaintances that can build us up or tear us down. Associating with the wrong crowd can take us in the wrong direction. Being with quality people who have Christian values can help make each of us a better person.

When I was in college at Tulane University, there were several different groups of people that I had a choice to spend time with. One group of friends spent much of their time focused on partying and having a good time, and they placed minimal emphasis on their future careers. Another group practiced their faith and occasionally attended parties but concentrated on their education in order to build career opportunities. After a while, it was clear that the Holy Spirit was guiding me to spend my time with those that valued their education and faith.

Once we reach our late teens or early twenties, we often become fully aware of how our family of origin, role models, and other associations have shaped us into the men or women that we are. As we move further along in life, we are further molded by our choices in marriage, the culture in which we work and live, and how we spend our free time. As you read this book, whether you are in your twenties, thirties, forties, fifties, sixties, or beyond, you can begin to understand the answers to these questions: "Why am I the person that I am?" and "How did I get to this point in my life?" All these influences have shaped us into the adults we have become.

Most importantly, you don't have to stay where you are. It is time to fly with the angels and soar with the saints to a happier, holier place in your life. Change is in the air, and it is happening to you by the grace of our Lord.

It Is Time for a Spiritual Self-Audit (SSA) to Identify the Issues that Rob Me of Happiness and Holiness

Many employers do an annual review of their employees. This review often includes a self-audit of an employee's performance. There are typical questions for this type of audit. Did you meet your sales goals? How did you add value to the business? Did your performance positively impact the reputation of the business in the community? Were you effective in managing others? In what ways did you impact the company morale? Employers use the self-audit process to help employees to continue to develop in their roles and to improve their performance in the business. Even professional sports teams do audits of team performance.

Sometimes, parents are forced to conduct a self-audit regarding their parenting skills. When a child comes home with a poor report card, or a parent-teacher conference reveals misconduct or sociability issues, parents may need to adjust. Through self-analysis, a parent can discern the changes that need to take place in their parenting in order to guide their child toward a successful academic career. These self-audits can be both very positive and painful.

Spiritual Excellence

Audits are common in all aspects of life, so why not a Spiritual Self-Audit (SSA) for your soul?

What is an SSA? This is an analysis of our individual performance in serving God. After all, we are in this life to serve Him, not to serve ourselves. This analysis may identify issues that rob us of our happiness and holiness and may further indicate why we experience stress, fear, anxiety, and worry.

An SSA requires thoughtful reflection on specific questions about our relationship with God and our daily actions:

Do I have more than one God in my life? Sometimes, we can allow the drive for material possessions to consume us. Perhaps you can't rest until you are driving a luxury car, living in a certain neighborhood, or have the latest technology or gadgets. A few years ago, I saw a bumper sticker which stated that the person who dies with the most toys is the winner. This is an ill-conceived message of greed. We can fall prey to the god of material things.

Why do I let fear, stress, worry, and anxiety consume me at times? Negative thoughts can control our lives if we let them.

What sinful ways or weaknesses do I have that work against God's teachings? These faults can include jealousy, anger, laziness, selfishness, slander, self-pride, lust, disrespect of others, hatred, and intentional harm to others. This list is not all-inclusive but reflects many of the issues that hurt our relationship with God and can rob us of peace and happiness.

Are there addictive behaviors that control my life? At times, we can struggle with self-discipline. Excessive consumption of food or alcohol, the use of recreational drugs, or viewing pornography, to name a few, rob us of our natural joy in life. Neither our bodies nor our minds are wired by Jesus for these addictive behaviors. There is no place for them in our world.

Am I practicing my faith by attending Mass and having a meaningful prayer life? We are often engaged in a battle for time. If we leave out time for prayer, spiritual reading, or frequent Mass attendance, we open ourselves to harmful influences which make us subject to fear, worry, and anxiety. Quality spiritual time management must be part of our daily plan in order to lay the foundation for strong faith.

In what ways am I fulfilling God's purpose for me on earth? In thinking about all the activities that I am involved with, am I serving as a disciple of God, or am I working for the evil one? In other words, who is my boss? Am I listening to the voice of God or the evil one?

Do I lead others to our Lord, or do I lead them astray? Often, we don't realize that our selfish actions are observed and followed by those around us. If we are practicing Christian values in the things that we do, we bring others closer to our Lord. By contrast, inappropriate conduct leads us and others in the wrong direction, works against our faith, and brings us closer to the evil one.

Am I sitting on the sidelines of life, or am I fully engaged in making a difference in the world? A friend once told me his daily focus is "to squeeze the juice out of life." In other words, to do all he can to make a difference for his family and for others. *Everyone* has time in their week to perform some type of ministry to benefit our Lord's people.

At the end of our earthly life, we will be judged according to the use of our time and talents. Will God say, "Well done, my good and faithful servant.... Come, share your master's joy" (Matt. 25:23)? Or will He say, "You wicked, lazy servant!... Throw this useless servant into the darkness outside, where there will be wailing and grinding of teeth" (Matt. 25:26, 30)? Judgment Day will come for all of us, when we will be face-to-face with God. When we see Him, we want to see a smile on His face acknowledging that we have served Him well.

It is time for each of us to do an SSA so that we can identify the weaknesses in our lives and correct them. We can't afford to procrastinate in doing an SSA. It takes only ten to fifteen minutes, time we could all find perhaps by giving up social media or television for just one night When our time in this life is over, we want God to say, "Well done, my good and faithful servant.... Come, share your master's joy."

Listed below are the issues to consider in your SSA. Check the issues that rob you of your happiness and holiness. Each issue corresponds to a chapter in Part II of this book that addresses the concern.

- Is my faith in doubt?
- What sinful ways, vices, or weaknesses do I have that work against God's teachings, such as jealousy, laziness, gluttony, hatred of others, substance abuse, slander, anger, lust, or disrespect toward others?
- Is my suffering managing me, or am I managing it?
- Do fear, stress, worry, and anxiety consume me at times?
- How do I handle conflict and adversity?

- Am I self-disciplined?
- Do I spend my money my way or God's way?
- How do I react when anger rears its ugly head?
- Does my self-pride make me think that I am better than others?
- Is it a challenge for me to forgive others?
- Am I selfish, thinking about myself and not others?
- Does poor spiritual time management limit my practice of the Faith?
- Do I focus more on my earthly retirement goals than on my goal of eternal salvation?

Now that you have checked off the issues that negatively affect you, go to the chapters in Part II that analyze them. Consider reading the other chapters in Part II that you didn't check off, as they may also be of help to you.

Part II

Analysis of the Issues Identified in Your Spiritual Self-Audit

Chapter 1

Why Is My Faith in Doubt?

In the early years of my law practice, I went to Alexandria, Louisiana, for a court conference in the summertime. The senior partner that I was assisting decided that we would fly to the conference on a chartered twin-engine prop plane. I had my doubts about flying in a small plane in Louisiana during the summer, as there are usually pop-up thunderstorms in the afternoon. Before we boarded the plane, our pilot, Ron, assured us that we would be safe. He said in response to my concerns that we would have "no problem."

The morning flight was smooth. But the return flight in the afternoon was another story. Twenty minutes into the afternoon flight, we looked out the window and saw ominous gray and black clouds all around and bolts of lightning. These weather conditions were not good. My worst fears were coming true.

My faith in Ron was in question. I asked Ron, "Are we going to be okay?" His response: "No problem." Not one minute later, we hit a pocket of air turbulence. The plane dropped in the sky, and our heads hit the ceiling. The senior partner slept through it all.

Again, I asked Pilot Ron, "How are we doing?" His response: "No problem." Shortly after, a lightning bolt snapped to the right of the plane, causing Ron to jerk the controls to the left. The other junior attorney on board and I grabbed each other's arm when the lightning flashed. We were scared. We began to pray. Fortunately, we landed safely, and I kissed the ground and thanked God for His protection. I looked at Pilot Ron. "No problem," he said. "Piece of cake."

Just as I needed to have faith in Pilot Ron on the flight that day, our Lord is calling us to have unwavering faith in Him.

Our Lord teaches us about the importance of faith in Him through the many miracles He performed during His earthly days. In chapter 5 of Mark's Gospel, Jesus raised a twelve-year-old girl from the dead and cured a woman afflicted with hemorrhages. In each instance, Jesus taught those present, and all of us today, about the importance of having faith in Him. The father of the girl was told that his daughter had died while he was in the presence of Jesus. Our Lord told him, "Do not be afraid, just have faith" (Mark 5:36).

Shortly thereafter, the young girl arose and began to walk. In the second miracle, a woman had been suffering from a blood disease for many years. She was treated by many doctors without success. Because of her faith, she touched our Lord's cloak, believing that by touching His clothes, she would be cured. After she was cured, Jesus told her, "Daughter, your faith has saved you. Go in peace and be cured of your affliction" (Mark 5:34).

In Matthew's Gospel, we also hear Jesus challenge the apostles to trust in Him. Jesus and the apostles were in a boat at sea when "suddenly a violent storm came up on the sea, so that the boat was being swamped by waves." Jesus was asleep and did not wake up at the time of the storm. The apostles woke Him, saying, "'Lord, save us! We are perishing!' He said to them, 'Why are you terrified, O you of little faith?' Then he got up, rebuked the winds and the sea, and there was great calm." The apostles were amazed and said, "What sort of man is this, whom even the winds and the sea obey?" (Matt. 8:23–27).

Jesus is unable to help those who either reject Him or have no faith in Him. Our Lord demonstrated this to us when He was unable to do mighty deeds in His hometown of Nazareth. The people there viewed Him as a lowly carpenter's son and did not have faith that He was the Savior. Our Lord commented about their lack of faith when He said, "A prophet is not without honor except in his native place and among his own kin and in his own house" (Mark 6:4).

In the world we live in, we often have to put our trust in people. We trust the hands of surgeons to save our lives or repair our bodies. We trust teachers to educate our children in subjects such as science, mathematics, and English in order to give them career opportunities. We trust electricians to repair problems in our homes and businesses and help prevent any type of electrical fires. We trust attorneys to give us sound advice on legal problems or enforce or defend our rights in a dispute. Since we put our full trust in people at times, why can't we have unwavering faith in God to help us with our concerns? So often, we try to solve issues that we face on our own. Our self-pride gets in the way. We adopt the attitude that we don't need Jesus, but come times of crisis, we beg His help.

The Gospels and the Acts of the Apostles reveal the transition of the apostles from cautionary acceptance to 100 percent unwavering faith in Jesus. During the three years before His Crucifixion, when the apostles were with Jesus, they had limited faith in Him. After our Lord was crucified, this limited trust was replaced by fear. Then after Jesus appeared to them and they received the power of the Holy Spirit, they transitioned to a state of unwavering trust. In fact, their faith was so strong that all but one of the apostles were crucified for their beliefs. St. Peter tells us that the genuineness of faith in God is more precious than gold (1 Pet. 1:6–7).

So where are we on the spectrum of faith in our Lord? Are we sometimes on the bottom end of the spectrum, which criticizes and rejects Jesus and maybe even works against Him? Are we in the middle, with limited faith and sometimes closed-mindedness? This can happen when we are suddenly faced with the loss of a job or a health crisis and we say, "Why me, Lord?" What about a financial crisis that arises, and we don't know where to turn for help, and we wonder if the crisis will work out? In some instances, when something negative happens, we abandon our faith altogether.

The challenge for us is to stay on the top end of the spectrum, with unwavering belief in Jesus at all times and in all situations. How can we not be on the top end of the spectrum after all the miracles He performed while on earth? Remember, our Lord proved He has control over all things, including life and death, by raising Lazarus from the dead in the presence of his sisters, Martha and Mary (John 11:1–44). After Lazarus had died and was buried, Jesus went to the tomb with Martha and Mary, and He spoke in a loud voice, "Lazarus, come out!" (John 1:43). At His command, Lazarus stepped out of the tomb.

Sometimes, we do not recognize that Our Lord has control over our lives when we fail to see the many small miracles He performs for us, including those that are physical, spiritual, psychological, emotional, or social. Think about the miracle of a healthy baby, cures for disease, and new medicines which give us better quality of life. We must always remember Our Lord's message to Martha at the time He raised Lazarus from the dead:

"I am the resurrection and the life; whoever believes in me, even if he dies, will live, and everyone who lives and believes in me will never die" (John 11:25–27).

Jesus further tells us in Matthew's Gospel, "Amen, I say to you, if you have faith, and do not waver, not only will you do what has been done to the fig tree, but even if you say to this mountain, 'Be lifted up and thrown into the sea,' it will be done" (Matt. 21:21). St. Augustine of Hippo (AD 354–430) tells us that "faith is to believe what we do not see; the reward of this faith is to see what we believe."[2]

Our Lord wants us to experience the fullness of the meaning of life and to put the power of faith at work in our lives. He knows each one of us and our needs. Remember from Mark's Gospel when the woman touched Jesus' cloak, her blood disease was cured. The miracle happened even though Jesus never saw or spoke to her before she was cured. He already knew her needs. The ultimate benefit from complete faith is getting to Heaven. Our Lord said, "Amen, amen, I say to you, whoever believes has eternal life" (John 6:47). Simply stated, our Lord is always there for us. We have to do our part by having unwavering faith in Him.

---

[2] Our Lady of Mercy Lay Carmelite Community #565, olmlay-carmelites.org.

Spiritual Treasures for Reflection

The genuineness of faith in God is more precious than gold. (see 1 Pet. 1:6–7)

"If you have faith and do not waiver, not only will you do what has been done to the fig tree, but even if you say to this mountain, 'Be lifted up and thrown into the sea,' it will be done." (Matt. 21:21)

"Amen, amen, I say to you, whoever believes has eternal life." (John 6:47)

Personal Notes of Reflection

_____

_____

_____

_____

_____

Chapter 2

Weapons against Temptation, Sin, and Vice

In Luke 4:1–13, after Jesus was baptized in the Jordan River, He went into the desert for forty days to fast. After completing His fasting, He was tempted by the devil several times. Jesus was encouraged by the devil to make bread out of stones to overcome His hunger. Then the devil offered Jesus power over all the kingdoms of the world in exchange for His allegiance. Finally, the devil urged Jesus to throw Himself off the top of the Temple to see if God's angels would catch Him. Our Lord was able to overcome these temptations by the grace of God, His Father. The temptation of Jesus by the devil in the desert was intended to compel Jesus to forgo His mission from God to be the Savior of the world.

The devil continues to operate in our world, seeking to entice all of us to commit sin and practice vices in order to separate us from Our Lord. He further wants to prevent us from doing our earthly mission from God. There are numerous temptations, sins, and vices that can invade our lives. Self-pride, jealousy, laziness, lust, disrespect of others, gluttony, hatred, slander, substance abuse, and impure thoughts are some of the sins that can consume us. Participating in this type of sinful conduct provides temporary self-pleasure. The evil one encourages us to engage in such behavior, but at some point, these actions will cause us to crash. A time will come when no one else is around, and we will reflect on the condition of our souls, and guilt will stare us in the face. It is difficult to shake this horrible feeling. We have robbed our souls of happiness and holiness by our actions.

In chapter 3 of St. Paul's Letter to the Colossians, he tells us how to change the course of this misconduct. He directs us to take off our old self with its ill practices and put on a new self that is renewed in the image of God. We must replace the vices that separate us from our Lord and replace them with patience, kindness, humility, gentleness, and heartfelt compassion. Furthermore, we are to bear with one another, forgive others, and, most of all, use love as the bond of perfection. By putting on a new self, we will experience peace by allowing Jesus to control our hearts. Lastly, St. Paul tells us to do everything in the name of the Lord Jesus.

Another way to think about the message from St. Paul is to replace vices with virtues. A virtue is defined as a habitual and firm disposition to do good. The virtuous person is one who freely practices doing good. See *Catechism of the Catholic Church* (hereafter, cited as CCC), paragraphs 1803 and 1804.

There are different types of virtues. The cardinal virtues are prudence, justice, fortitude, and temperance. Prudence allows us to determine true good in every situation and to choose the right way of achieving it. Justice is the "constant and firm will to give their due to God and neighbor." Fortitude strengthens our resolve to resist temptations and gives us firmness in managing difficulties and constancy in the pursuit of good. Temperance provides mastery over instincts and keeps our desires under control (CCC 1805–1809).

The theological virtues relate directly to God and allow us to participate in the divine nature. These virtues of faith, hope, and charity permit us to live in a relationship with the Holy Trinity. They are the foundation of Christian moral activity (CCC 1812–1813). For many of us, changing our ways of ill practices and becoming renewed in the image of God by utilizing virtues may not be as easy as flipping on a light switch. St. Ignatius of Loyola gave us a process to make this change by performing a daily examination of our consciences. This process calls us to evaluate our performance in serving Our Lord each day and to see where He was active in our lives. This prayer can be accomplished by following these simple steps. First, acknowledge that you are in the presence of God. Then think about ways that you were blessed by Him. Next, examine your day from start to finish, thinking about the times when God was present for you in both small and large things. Then express sorrow to Him for any sins you have committed and seek forgiveness. Finally, seek grace from God for the next day.[3]

After a few days of engaging in a daily examination of conscience, it is likely that any patterns of harmful misconduct will become obvious. Our souls will be totally embarrassed before Our Lord because of our behavior. We will recognize that we must terminate the vices and replace them with virtues. This will restore happiness in our lives.

To further support our efforts to overcome temptation and sin, Jesus provides us with grace. Our Lord's "gift of salvation offers us the grace necessary to persevere in the pursuit of the virtues" (CCC 1811). Grace is readily available to us. All we have to do is ask our Lord and Savior for it in prayer. Best of all, grace is free. There is no charge. During His ministry on earth, Jesus gave us a prayer to say to His Father to help us overcome

[3]   The Ignatian Examen, Jesuits.org.

temptation. In the Lord's Prayer, we ask God, "Do not subject us to the final test, but deliver us from the evil one" (Matt. 6:13).

In John's Gospel, Jesus speaks with the apostles and disciples about various spiritual matters. He instructs them in simple terms about the end result of sinful misconduct compared to a life of following His ways. The Spirit leads to eternal life, while the sinfulness of the flesh is of no avail (John 6:63). We all know the challenges of temptation and sin in this earthly life. Sometimes, we feel that we are in a tug of war between vices and virtues. However, in our hearts, we know that virtues must always triumph. Virtues, God's grace, and prayer are our weapons against temptation, sin, and vice.

Spiritual Treasures for Reflection

Take off your old self with its ill practices and put on a new self, renewed in the image of God. (see Col. 3:9–10)

"A virtue is an habitual and firm disposition to do good." (CCC 1803)

Our Lord's "gift of salvation offers us the grace necessary to persevere in the pursuit of the virtues." (CCC 1811)

"And do not subject us to the final test, but deliver us from the evil one." (Matt. 6:13)

Personal Notes of Reflection

_____

_____

_____

_____

_____

Chapter 3

Tools to Handle Suffering

Ashley Code was an excellent student at Mount Carmel Academy in New Orleans. In the summer of 2015, she was diagnosed with an inoperable brain tumor and was in a coma for six days. Thereafter, Ashley began intense treatment for the tumor, including radiation and chemotherapy. While she was in treatment, Sr. Camille Anne Campbell, the principal of the school, said, "I am so sorry this is happening to you." In response, Ashley said, "Jesus suffered, Sister. It's okay." During this time of intense suffering, Ashley did all that she could to care for others by doing acts of kindness and demonstrating great love, joy, and peace. She was selfless during these hard times.

Suffering is a part of life. Our Lord gives us the tools to manage any type of suffering, whether it is physical, mental, spiritual, social, or emotional. He showed us these tools through the way He managed His own suffering.

So what are the tools that Jesus gives us to manage suffering?

Obedience. Our Lord was obedient to the Father. Jesus knew the kind of suffering He would experience before it happened. He said to His apostles, "The Son of Man must suffer greatly and be rejected by the elders, the chief priests, and the scribes, and be killed and on the third day be raised" (Luke 9:22). He embraced His wrongful conviction, torture, and Crucifixion, as this was the will of His Father. Jesus willingly accepted His Passion, freeing us from the Original Sin of Adam and Eve. We, too, can manage our suffering by embracing and accepting the will of Jesus for us.

Be selfless. Try to be selfless and caring for others when facing suffering. While carrying the Cross on His way to His Crucifixion, and in intense pain, Jesus comforted the crowds who followed Him, saying, "Daughters of Jerusalem, do not weep for me" (Luke 23:28). When nailed to the Cross, Jesus consoled a criminal who was hanging next to Him, saying, "Amen, I say to you, today you will be with Me in paradise" (Luke 23:43). If we focus on others, then we think less about our own suffering.

Do not complain. Jesus demonstrated great spiritual strength, self-discipline, and peace despite His intense suffering. He never complained about the pain or showed fear or anxiety. He was strong like a rock and was a model for us all.

Prayer. Jesus prayed daily to His Father when He was in this life, especially during His suffering. The elements of a strong prayer life are very simple: be humble of heart with no expectation, be patient, be persistent, have unwavering faith in His merciful love for us, and be thankful to our Lord for listening to our prayers. There are many kinds of prayers to consider, including praying for others, discussing your day with Jesus, traditional rote prayers, prayerful reading of Scripture, prayers with others, keeping a personal journal, and invoking the aid of our Blessed Mother Mary and the saints. The fruits of a dedicated and focused prayer life are awesome. They include true joy and happiness despite suffering, daily direction in all decision-making, courage to handle any adversity, unlimited graces, and self-discipline. But most of all, the greatest fruit is the chance to be in Heaven with our Lord.

Forgive. Forgive those who cause us to suffer. Our Lord utilized forgiveness as another way to manage suffering. While hanging on the Cross, He asked God to forgive those who tortured Him, saying, "Father, forgive them, they know not what they do" (Luke 23:34). Resentment can be detrimental to our emotional state, and forgiveness can eliminate it. Jesus summarized His teachings about handling suffering. "If anyone wishes to come after me, he must deny himself and take up his cross daily and follow me. For whoever wishes to save his life will lose it, but whoever loses his life for my sake will save it" (Luke 9:23–24).

God gives us all the grace we need to handle suffering. St. Paul reminds us of this grace in his Letter to the Corinthians: "No trial has come to you but what is human. God is faithful and will not let you be tried beyond your strength; but with the trial he will also provide a way out, so that you may be able to bear it" (1 Cor. 10:13).

Many saints show us comforting ways to manage suffering. St. Thérèse of Lisieux said, "My God, I choose all. I don't want to be a saint by halves. I'm not afraid to suffer for You, I fear only one thing: to keep my own will. So take it, for I choose all that You will."[4]

St. Peter tells us, "Beloved, do not be surprised that a trial by fire is occurring among you, as if something strange were happening to you. But rejoice to the extent that you share in the sufferings of Christ, so that when His glory is revealed you may also rejoice exultantly" (1 Pet. 4:12–13).

Pope St. John Paul II discussed suffering this way:

> The Redeemer suffered in place of man and for man. Every man *has his own share in the Redemption*. Each one is also *called to share in that suffering* through which ... all human suffering has also been redeemed. In bringing about the Redemption through suffering, Christ *has* also *raised human suffering to the level of Redemption*. Thus each man, in his suffering, can also become a sharer in the redemptive suffering of Christ.[5]

When can we use the tools Jesus gave us to withstand suffering? One of these times is when we experience the death of a loved one. We need to be spiritually strong and at peace in order to support our family during this time of loss, confident that our Lord is taking care of the loved one. When my father's last brother died, I asked him how he handled it so well. He said, "I have got to be a rock for the family."

The loss of a job or key customer can bring suffering. We need to be obedient to Jesus and His ways and rely upon divine

---

4   *Story of a Soul: The Autobiography of St. Thérèse of Lisieux*, trans. John Clarke, O.C.D., 2nd ed. (Washington, DC: ICS Publications, 1976), 27.

5   John Paul II. Apostolic Letter *Salvifici Doloris* (February 1984), no. 19.

providence that a new opportunity will come our way. When our Lord closes one door, He will open another. St. Mother Théodore Guérin came from France to southern Indiana in the 1850s with the assignment to start a school system from scratch. She knew no one and had little money. Relying upon divine providence from God, she started her first school. Then sixteen others followed. She was obedient to the will of God and embraced His mission for her.

There will be other times when we experience physical, psychological, emotional, or social suffering. When this happens, it is important to be selfless by demonstrating love for others who are concerned for us. St. Teresa Benedicta of the Cross was brought to a concentration camp by the Nazis during World War II to be murdered in the gas chambers. She spent her last days comforting all those around her in total selflessness. St. Teresa Benedicta said, "Until this hour, You have not delivered me from sorrow. Sometimes its weight on me is great. Yet You give me strength and so I bear it. Bless me now as I sleep. Be mindful of Your own Son's agony in His death's hour. And to the dead, grant peace."[6]

In other instances, we can be wrongly criticized by others or bullied because of our beliefs. When this happens, always remember what Jesus told us. "Blessed are you when they insult you and persecute you and utter every kind of evil against you [falsely] because of me. Rejoice and be glad, for your reward will be great in heaven" (Matt. 5:11–12). We can't allow the negatives that can come with suffering and tough times to influence us. Some of these negatives include anger, the desire for retaliation, self-pity,

---

[6]   Waltraud Herbstrith, *Edith Stein: A Victim of the Shoah* (Eckbolsheim: Editions du Signe, 2004).

blaming others, or being selfish. These negatives have no place in our lives. When these feelings occur, we have a choice either to join our Lord's mission on earth or to work against Him. We are working for Jesus when we utilize the tools He gave us for handling our suffering. We are working against Jesus when we feel sorry for ourselves, become angry, blame others, are selfish, or seek retaliation. Suffering and tough times force us to rise to the occasion to live as the saints have done.

These challenges can purify the sinful tendencies in our human will. Old school football coaches describe the response to these challenges using the expression "When the going gets tough, the tough get going."

There are those around us who are role models for accepting their cross of suffering. My father was a faithful follower of our Lord. He attended Mass daily, was very active in our church parish, and had a great relationship with our Blessed Mother Mary. On December 6, 1993, my Pop was in the hospital suffering from heart disease and diabetes. Both his legs had been amputated, he previously had open heart surgery, and he was being fed through a tube. When I visited him that night, I left very sad, knowing that our Lord was probably going to call him from this life soon. When I got home that night, he called me on the telephone and said in a weak voice, "Don't worry, son, I am okay. I am not going tonight." My Pop cared about me despite his great suffering. He died two days later, on December 8, 1993, the Feast of the Immaculate Conception of Our Lady.

Another role model for me was Joyce, a patient at a nursing home in New Orleans. For several years, she suffered from multiple sclerosis and was confined to a wheelchair. Despite her great suffering, she was always cheerful. Joyce had a big smile on her face, telling everyone to have a great day. She used to say,

"This is the day the Lord has made." Joyce was always helping other patients by comforting them and calling for assistance for them when needed. She fully accepted her suffering, never complained, and always found ways to bring others closer to Jesus by her great attitude. When I would bring the Eucharist to her at the nursing home, she would always say that without her Catholic faith, she couldn't make it each day. Joyce was a ray of sunshine in a tough place where the majority of patients were suffering greatly.

We began this chapter by writing about Ashley Code, a student at Mt. Carmel Academy. Ashley was only seventeen years old when our Lord called her home. During her short life, she taught us so much about how to use the tools Jesus gave us to handle suffering. She was obedient to the will of God and embraced her suffering. After passing, Ashley's friends said that she was selfless and would forever live on in their memories because of her good deeds. She taught them, through faith in Christ, that all things are possible, and that Jesus is always here to help us and lighten the load.

Spiritual Treasures for Reflection

"Jesus suffered, Sister. It's okay." (Ashley Code)

"If anyone wishes to come after me, he must deny himself and take up his cross daily and follow me. For whoever wishes to save his life will lose it, but whoever loses his life for my sake will save it." (Luke 9:23–24)

"No trial has come to you but what is human. God is faithful and will not let you be tried beyond your strength; but with the trial he will also provide a way out, so that you may be able to bear it." (1 Cor. 10:13)

"My God, I choose all. I don't want to be a saint by halves. I'm not afraid to suffer for You, I fear only one thing: to keep my own will. So take it, for I choose all that You will." (St. Thérèse of Lisieux)

Personal Notes of Reflection

_____

_____

_____

_____

_____

Chapter 4

When Fear, Stress, Worry, and Anxiety Meet Courage, Faith, and Peace

Part of my grammar school education was spent at Christian Brothers School, located in City Park, New Orleans. At that time, the whole faculty was composed of Christian Brothers who were well known as great educators of boys and as strict disciplinarians. You truly could hear a pin drop in the classrooms. One of the ways used by the brothers to enforce discipline was to assign memorandums to students who misbehaved in class. A dreaded memo assignment was to write about life inside of a ping-pong ball.

At eleven years old, you can only imagine how challenging this assignment was, especially because we had to produce five hundred words on the subject. The obvious point to discuss was the physical impact of being bounced around inside the ball by the ping-pong players. Other points were less obvious, such as being bounced around by the stress and worry to earn great grades, gain the respect of your fellow students, and maintain proper conduct in the classroom. The goal of the brothers in issuing these assignments was to improve our behavior in school and to teach us to think about some of the basic issues in life.

Spiritual Excellence

Life for us in America today often feels like we are being bounced around inside a ping-pong ball because of fear, stress, worry, and anxiety. These negative symptoms rob us of our happiness. Why can't we change this way of life by replacing these symptoms with courage, faith, and peace? The simple answer to the question is that we can make the choice each day to live a life that restores our natural happiness. We can step outside of the ping-pong ball effects of fear, stress, worry, and anxiety. A remedy for these emotions is courage. The word courage is often described as the strength, mental or moral, to handle fear and struggles. Synonyms for courage are tenacity, resilience, and determination. Surely, we can swap the negative symptoms of fear, stress, and worry with a self-prescribed dose of courage, faith, and peace.

In Matthew's Gospel, we read about the story of Peter walking on water. After Jesus performed a miracle by providing enough fish and bread to feed five thousand people, He told His disciples to get into a boat and go to the other side of the sea. After doing so, Jesus went up the mountain to pray by Himself. As the apostles were sailing several miles from shore, high winds and waves tossed their boat around. In the midst of their ordeal, Jesus began walking on the sea toward them. The apostles saw Him and "they were terrified. 'It is a ghost,' they said, and they cried out in fear. At once [Jesus] spoke to them, 'Take courage, it is I; do not be afraid.' Peter said to him in reply, 'Lord, if it is you, command me to come to you on the water.' He said, 'Come.' Peter got out of the boat and began to walk on the water toward Jesus" (Matt. 14:26–29). But Peter started sinking as fear overcame him. Immediately, Jesus reached out and caught Peter.

In this story, the apostle Peter experienced two rounds of fear and courage on the stormy sea that night. In each round, he eventually abandoned fear and replaced it with courage. Peter first experienced fear when he saw Jesus but thought He was a ghost. Once he realized the figure on the water was Jesus, he found his courage. Subsequently, Peter was fearful when he walked on the water. His lack of faith caused him to sink. Once Jesus reached out and gave Peter His hand, Peter regained his courage. Peter's courage on the stormy sea resulted from his complete focus on our Lord. Such focus can help us to live in a state of courage, destroying any possible fear, stress, or worry. When Peter kept his attention fixed on Jesus, he was able to handle his troubles. Focusing all our attention on Jesus is the difference between sinking in the waves of life or walking on the top of the challenges we face.

New Orleans Archbishop Gregory Aymond addressed the issue of fear and worry this way. Early in his career, he was the rector at Notre Dame Seminary. During his tenure, he often served Sunday Mass at our home parish of St. Ann. Every Mass, Archbishop Aymond would ask our Lord to keep us from useless worry, fear, and stress. He knew these negative symptoms were harming us, and he invoked our Lord to come to our aid.

There are times when we have a choice to make between fear and courage. A deacon friend of mine was diagnosed with cancer several years ago. He prayed to Jesus for the grace of courage to handle the treatment and the outcome. My friend's cancer is in remission, and he is doing a fabulous job serving Jesus as a deacon. He received the grace of courage to withstand his worst fears.

Facing a medical procedure is not the only time we must choose courage over worry. We need it when we are starting a new business or career, changing jobs, parenting our children, taking a stand against immoral issues or unethical business practices, defending a co-worker despite knowing we will suffer for it, going forward in life after losing a spouse, family member, or close friend, or going to a new school. This list is by no means exhaustive but represents the types of issues that can require courage.

Our Lord further teaches us that in addition to courage, faith can help us counter fear, stress, and worry. We need to have faith in God, because He exercises control over everything in the world, which includes our individual needs. Our Lord says,

> Therefore I tell you, do not worry about your life, what you will eat [or drink], or about your body, what you will wear. Is not life more than food and the body more than clothing? Look at the birds in the sky; they do not sow or reap, they gather nothing into barns, yet your heavenly Father feeds them. Are not you more important than they? Can any of you by worrying add a single moment to your life-span? Why are you anxious about clothes? Learn from the way the wild flowers grow. They do not work or spin. But I tell you that not even Solomon in all his splendor was clothed like one of them. If God so clothes the grass of the field, which grows today and is thrown into the oven tomorrow, will He not much more provide for you, O you of little faith? So do not worry and say, 'What are we to eat?' Or 'What are we to drink?' Or 'What are we to wear?' All these things the pagans seek. Your heavenly Father knows that you need them all. But seek first the kingdom [of God] and His righteousness, and all these things will be given you besides. (Matt. 6:25–33)

Salomone LeClercq was born in France in 1745. At the age of twenty-two, he entered the Institute of the Brothers of the

Christian Schools. He began his career as a Christian Brother, teaching in France and later became the provincial superior of the order. In 1790, during the French Revolution, Br. Salomone demonstrated great faith when he refused to take the oath of allegiance to the new French governor. His allegiance was to Jesus. Because of his faith, he was arrested and imprisoned at a Carmelite convent in Paris. Nearly three weeks after his arrest, he was stabbed to death in the garden of the convent by French revolutionaries. Pope Francis canonized him as a saint on October 16, 2016, in St. Peter's Square.

We can utilize peace to overcome stress and anxiety as well. Our Lord offers us divine peace when He tells us, "Peace I leave with you; my peace I give to you. Not as the world gives do I give it to you. Do not let your hearts be troubled or afraid" (John 14:27). After Jesus died, the apostles experienced great fear because their Lord and Savior had been crucified. They had no direction and were worried that they would be executed like Him. Shortly thereafter, the Holy Spirit descended upon the apostles, and they received the virtues of peace, faith, and courage (John 20:19–23; Mark 16:14–18). They became miracle workers for those suffering physically and spiritually. After many years in ministry spreading Christianity, all of the remaining apostles but one were martyred. Without these virtues, the apostles could not have withstood this type of passion and death.

In the game of baseball, coaches are always giving instructions to their hitters. One of them is to "keep your eye on the ball at all times." We can all experience an end to fear, stress, worry, and anxiety if we follow the teachings of Jesus and the examples of His apostles and saints. These negative symptoms can be replaced by courage, faith, and peace by keeping our eye on Jesus and His ways.

Spiritual Treasures for Reflection

"Take courage, it is I; do not be afraid." (Matt. 14:27)

"Do not worry and say, 'What are we to eat?' or 'What are we to drink?' or 'What are we to wear?' All these things the pagans seek. Your heavenly Father knows that you need them all. But seek first the kingdom [of God] and His righteousness, and all these things will be given you besides." (Matt. 6:31–33)

"Peace I leave with you; my peace I give to you. Not as the world gives do I give it to you. Do not let your hearts be troubled or afraid." (John 14:27)

Personal Notes of Reflection

_____

_____

_____

_____

_____

Chapter 5

Handling Conflict and Adversity

Malala Yousafzai was a student at a public school when the Taliban took over her hometown of Mingora, Pakistan. The Taliban threatened to blow up her all-girl school and ordered all teachers to wear all-encompassing burkas. Malala responded by speaking out against the Taliban and championing girls' rights to education through television interviews. The Taliban retaliated and shot her in the head. After many surgeries, Malala survived and was awarded the Nobel Peace Prize at the age of seventeen. When faced with adversity, Malala responded by pursuing her rights in a peaceful way.

During Jesus' life on earth, He experienced frequent conflict and adversity from the time of His birth until His death. Through His experiences, He taught us how to peacefully handle conflict and adversity inflicted by others. Very powerful leaders were plotting against Jesus throughout His life. Shortly after He was born, King Herod wanted Jesus killed because he feared that our Lord would take over his kingdom (Matt. 2:1–13). Later in our Lord's life, when He was in the desert fasting, the devil wanted Jesus to give up His mission on earth to save our souls and offered Him all the kingdoms of the world in exchange for His allegiance (Matt. 4:1–11).

Spiritual Excellence

Even the Pharisees and Herodians feared Jesus, who was preaching to the people through parables. Our Lord was a threat to their power and their control over the people because He was converting many of them to His ways. In order to trick Jesus, they asked Him, "Is it lawful to pay the census tax to Caesar or not?" (Matt. 22:17).

Our Lord showed us the way to respond to adversity and conflict by His response to His enemies. He didn't scream and yell, resort to physical violence, or retaliate against them. Instead, He faced His adversaries courageously. Jesus relied upon the Holy Spirit and the angels for guidance and direction.

When King Herod sent troops to kill Jesus shortly after He was born, an angel appeared to Joseph and told him to go to Egypt to keep our Lord safe (Matt. 2:13–15). Later, before Jesus entered His Galilean ministry, He received guidance and wisdom from the Holy Spirit when He was tempted by the devil in the desert. Jesus said to the devil, "The Lord, your God, shall you worship and him alone shall you serve" (Matt. 4:10). Also, during His public ministry, to avoid the trap by the Pharisees and Herodians, the Holy Spirit guided Jesus to respond to their trick question this way: "Repay to Caesar what belongs to Caesar and to God what belongs to God" (Matt. 22:21).

There are other Scripture passages that give us guidance in handling conflict and adversity through perseverance and conviction. "Consider it all joy, my brothers, when you encounter various trials, for you know that the testing of your faith produces perseverance. And let perseverance be perfect, so that you may be perfect and complete, lacking in nothing" (James 1:2–4). St. Paul also tells us that the Holy Spirit is there for us with much conviction to handle adverse situations (1 Thess. 1:5–6).

St. Rita of Cascia was born in 1381 and experienced many tragic events in her lifetime. These included an arranged marriage at a young age to a cruel man who was later murdered by an enemy, the death of her two sons, several rejections in her attempt to gain entrance to the Augustinian convent before finally being accepted, frequent illness, and an open wound on her forehead that wouldn't heal. Conflict and adversity were almost a never-ending battle for St. Rita. Despite these challenges, she never lost her faith in God. She persevered through them with much conviction and received guidance from the Holy Spirit to handle her circumstances. St. Rita is known as the saint of impossible causes. Countless miracles have occurred through her intercession to our Lord.

Sometimes, we encounter individuals who cause our adversity, conflict, or heartache. There are times when brothers and sisters plot against each other over a family inheritance or desire for parental favoritism. Other times, bosses or co-workers step on us for their own gain, resulting in our loss of a job, position, or money. In some instances, business partners are overcome by greed or power and steal from each other. Even our friends can make fun of us or take advantage of our sincerity and generosity. How are we going to respond to this adversity, conflict, or heartache? We can't resort to violence, anger, or retaliation against our adversaries, nor can we hide or run away. We must face the challenges just as our Lord did. Through prayer, the Holy Spirit will give us the perseverance, conviction, and knowledge we need in order to have wisdom, calmness, and direction to handle the situation. Our response must be a reflection of our Lord's values rather than satisfaction of our ego to retaliate against those who hurt us.

Several years ago, I was taken advantage of in a real estate transaction and was very upset at the time. The Holy Spirit gave me the wisdom to withdraw my challenge to the action of my business colleague. I learned that my colleague needed the money much more than I did at the time. Admittedly, this was a tough pill to swallow back then, but the wisdom from the Holy Spirit gave me great acceptance and peace. We can't let conflict and adversity rob us of our joy in life. We must let the Holy Spirit guide and direct us when we are faced with these obstacles. We need to persevere through them with much conviction and calmness.

Spiritual Treasures for Reflection

"Consider it all joy, my brothers, when you encounter various trials, for you know that the testing of your faith produces perseverance. And let perseverance be perfect, so that you may be perfect and complete, lacking in nothing." (James 1:2–4)

The Holy Spirit is there for us with much conviction to handle adverse situations. (see 1 Thess. 1:5–6)

Personal Notes of Reflection

_____

_____

_____

_____

_____

Chapter 6

Where Did My Self-Discipline Go?

Championship teams in all sports at all levels have one thing in common: self-discipline. From high school volleyball teams to professional football teams, self-discipline is a key ingredient for success. This critical component is necessary for eating habits, practice effort, off-field conduct, and injury treatment. Also, in order to win games, players must exercise self-discipline on every play and in all situations both individually and as a team. Oftentimes, the difference between winning and losing is based on a missed tackle, a position mistake by a player on the court, or a foul. Great coaches constantly preach self-discipline to their players. Likewise, self-discipline is a critical component of our spiritual lives in order to serve our Lord and gain Heaven. We must have strong spiritual self-discipline.

At times, we can all struggle with spiritual self-discipline. We often think or act in earthly ways and not in God's ways. Laziness is a good example. We simply don't do the things we ought to be doing for ourselves, for our family and friends, or in our jobs. Overeating and excessive alcohol consumption can be a struggle for many. Even our spouse and children can suffer when we are undisciplined and fail to take care of household duties. Sometimes, we lose our patience with our children who are misbehaving or who are not taking care of their responsibilities. Spouses can become angry with one another over simple things. Our Lord tells us how to develop the spiritual self-discipline we need in order to be His disciples. He says, "Whoever wishes to come after, me must deny himself, take up his cross, and follow me" (Matt. 16:24). There are several components to this teaching.

First, Jesus tells us that we must deny ourselves to instill spiritual self-discipline. How do we do this? We deny ourselves by putting the needs of others before our own. This means always being available for our children by helping them do their homework, by going to their ball games and performances, and by praying with them at night — even though we may be exhausted. In the home, consider the needs of the family, such as shopping, meal preparation, and cleaning, before personal time. Also, always be willing to listen when a family member needs a sympathetic ear. In our daily habits, we need self-discipline to take proper care of ourselves by eating right, exercising our bodies, and refraining from excess consumption of food and alcohol.

The second component of spiritual self-discipline stated by Jesus in Matthew's Gospel is the command to take up our cross or challenges daily (Matt. 16:24). This is a willingness to accept trials that come our way, such as pain and suffering, hardships, humiliation because of our Christian values and beliefs, the passing of family members or friends, or the loss of a personal relationship.

The last component from this Scripture passage tells us to be proactive and follow Jesus. Think about what our Lord would do in any situation. Remember those wristbands that say, "What would Jesus do?" Simply pause before making a decision or speaking and consider how our Lord would handle the situation. This will give us the peace and confidence to do His will.

There are other biblical figures who provide guidance on this issue of spiritual self-discipline. St. Paul, who wrote thirteen books in the New Testament, speaks about the issue this way: "Do not conform yourselves to this age but be transformed by the renewal of your mind, that you may discern what is the will of God, what is good and pleasing and perfect" (Rom. 12:2).

Our first pope, St. Peter, learned spiritual self-discipline through his life experiences. His journey is well documented in the Gospels. At times, he denied even knowing Jesus (Luke 22:54–62, Mark 14:66–72, John 18:15–18, 25–27). In other situations, he lacked faith in God (Matt. 14:22–33). However, spiritual self-discipline later became a way of life for St. Peter after our Lord blessed him and the other apostles with the gifts and fruits of the Holy Spirit at Pentecost. Peter tells us, "Like obedient children, do not act in compliance with the desires of your former ignorance but, as he who called you is holy, be holy yourselves in every aspect of your conduct" (1 Pet. 1:14–15).

In the modern era, St. Thérèse of Lisieux explains our Lord's command for spiritual self-discipline in the context of becoming a saint. We must be willing to suffer much, deny our very selves, and always seek out the most perfect thing to do. Our focus must be on doing the will of our Lord 100 percent of the time.[7]

The Church helps us develop and maintain spiritual self-discipline. Through regular attendance at Mass, we are reminded of the great spiritual self-discipline of Jesus, even to the point of His Crucifixion on the Cross. By participating in the Sacrament of Confession at least monthly, we examine our consciences and admit where we have failed to exercise spiritual self-discipline

---

[7] *Story of a Soul*, 27.

and have committed sins. The Ten Commandments give us further direction.

How important is it for us to regain our spiritual self-discipline? Jesus tells us, "For whoever wishes to save his life will lose it, but whoever loses his life for my sake will find it. What profit would there be for one to gain the whole world and forfeit his life?... For the Son of Man will come with His angels in His Father's glory, and then He will repay everyone according to his conduct" (Matt. 16:25–27). In simple terms, just as sports teams win championships through individual self-discipline, souls gain Heaven by following God's ways through a life of spiritual self-discipline.

Spiritual Treasures for Reflection

"Whoever wishes to come after me must deny himself, take up his cross, and follow me." (Matt. 16:24)

"Do not conform yourselves to this age but be transformed by the renewal of your mind, that you may discern what is the will of God, what is good and pleasing and perfect." (Rom. 12:2)

"Like obedient children, do not act in compliance with the desires of your former ignorance but, as He who called you is holy, be holy yourselves in every aspect of your conduct." (1 Pet. 1:14–15)

Personal Notes of Reflection

_____

_____

_____

_____

_____

Chapter 7

Greed: Whose Money Is It Anyway—God's or Yours?

Thibodaux lived on a bayou in South Louisiana. He spent his life fishing and hunting and accumulating all kinds of wealth. He was very successful in his efforts. Thibodaux had a big house, fancy cars, several boats, a fabulous hunting camp, valuable jewelry, and millions of dollars in the bank. He told his wife, Clotilde, that when he died, he wanted to take his money with him. When Thibodaux passed away, Clotilde honored her husband's wishes. She put a check for the millions in his coffin.

Just as this joke illustrates, we all know you cannot take it with you. Despite this truth, our American culture encourages us to spend our time gathering great wealth. Remember the popular expression that says that the person who dies with the most toys wins? The goal of wealth accumulation often leads to greed. Greed is an intense and selfish desire for something such as wealth. It can consume our lives and dominate our daily activities. The desire for luxury cars, the latest technology, multiple homes, a huge bank account, and a large financial portfolio can be a detriment to us. Greed can be harmful to our families, our health, and our relationship with our friends, colleagues, and, most importantly, God.

Spiritual Excellence

Our Lord sets the record straight on the issue of greed. Jesus gives us the parable of the rich man and Lazarus. The rich man had the best clothes and ate delicious food each day. A poor man named Lazarus, who was covered in sores, was lying at the door of the home of the rich man. He was so hungry that he would have eaten the scraps from the rich man's table. When Lazarus died, he was brought by the angels to the bosom of Abraham. When the rich man died, he was brought to the netherworld, where he lived in flaming torment:

> He raised his eyes and saw Abraham far off and Lazarus at his side. And he cried out, "Father Abraham, have pity on me. Send Lazarus to dip the tip of his finger in water and cool my tongue, for I am suffering torment in these flames." Abraham replied, "My child, remember that you received what was good during your lifetime while Lazarus likewise received what was bad; but now he is comforted here, whereas you are tormented. Moreover, between us and you a great chasm is established to prevent anyone from crossing who might wish to go from our side to yours or from your side to ours." (Luke 16:23–26)

Then the rich man asked Abraham to send Lazarus to warn his five brothers so they could avoid the torment he was experiencing:

> But Abraham replied, "They have Moses and the prophets. Let them listen to them." He said, "Oh no, father Abraham, but if someone from the dead goes to them, they will repent." Then Abraham said, "If they will not listen to Moses and the prophets, neither will they be persuaded if someone should rise from the dead." (Luke 16:29–31)

It is important to point out that the rich man has no name in this parable. Think about it. Is it appropriate to plug in your own name as the rich man?

Jesus addresses the issue of greed more directly in Mark's Gospel. In this Scripture passage, a man came up to our Lord and said, "Good teacher, what must I do to inherit eternal life?" (Mark 10:17). Jesus told him to keep the commandments, and He further replied, "Go, sell what you have, and give to [the] poor and you will have treasure in heaven; then come, follow me" (Mark 10:21). After hearing these words, the man went away disheartened because he had many possessions. "Jesus looked around and said to his disciples, 'How hard it is for those who have wealth to enter the Kingdom of God!... It is easier for a camel to pass through [the] eye of a needle than for one who is rich to enter the kingdom of God" (Mark 10:23–25).

Pope Francis is a great role model for us in many ways. He shows us the way to lead a simple lifestyle by having limited possessions. The pope doesn't live in a fancy residence in the Vatican. He chooses to live in a guesthouse there and drives a car that is over twenty years old.

So whose money is it, anyway? Is it God's or yours? Think about the issue this way. For those who have accumulated wealth or who are working for it now, do we really think we are doing it all on our own? What if, instead of living in the United States, you were living in an impoverished country, where the focus of your daily activities was to find food and water for your family? Just consider who blessed you with the opportunity to live in the United States, where most enjoy great health and have a good job. This all comes from our Lord. This didn't happen because we did it ourselves. So whose money is it? Of course, it is God's. In acknowledging that the things we accumulate come from and belong to God, we need to use them as He would—wisely.

We can avoid greed by practicing good spiritual time management. This means spending an appropriate amount of time serving your family, doing ministry service for our Lord, and earning an income for your needs. Also, share your income with others, including the poor, your family and friends, and the Church. Leading a simpler lifestyle with fewer earthly things and sharing your resources will ensure great joy and happiness for you and your family.

St. Katharine Drexel is a good example of someone who used God's money wisely. She was born in Philadelphia, Pennsylvania, in 1858 and grew up in a wealthy family. She inherited a fortune in 1885. Instead of living a life of luxury, St. Katharine dedicated herself to her faith and to using her wealth to help the poor. She founded the religious order known as the Sisters of the Blessed Sacrament. She opened schools for African and Native American children in different parts of the United States, including Xavier University of New Orleans. St. Katharine was very frugal. She used pencils down to the stub. This wonderful saint used God's money wisely for the benefit of others.

St. Teresa of Calcutta was another role model for being frugal. Monsignor Christopher Nalty spent a summer with the Sisters of Charity while he was in the seminary. On his first morning there, he attended Mass with St. Teresa. In the chapel, there was only an altar and a few chairs for the celebrants. All those who attended Mass sat on the floor, as there was no other furniture in the chapel. Members of the order that she founded have very few possessions, which consist of three saris and a crucifix. The saris are made by lepers who are being cared for by the sisters.

In Luke's Gospel, Jesus again tells us about the ownership of wealth. In this parable, the prosperous man is pondering what to do with all of his wealth. He says, " 'Now as for you, you have so many good things stored up for many years, rest, eat, drink, be merry!' But God says to him, 'You fool, this night your life will be demanded of you; and the things you have prepared, to whom will they belong?' " The parable continues with the statement, "Thus will it be for the one who stores up treasure for himself but is not rich in what matters to God" (Luke 12:19–21).

The Old Testament book of Proverbs offers great wisdom on the issue of greed. "A good name is more desirable than great riches, and high esteem, than gold and silver" (Prov. 22:1). Furthermore, we are told, "Honor the Lord with your wealth, with first fruits of all your produce; Then will your barns be filled with grain, with new wine your vats will overflow" (Prov. 3:9–10).

Our Lord summed up the whole issue of greed in one sentence when He said, "What profit is there for one to gain the whole world yet lose or forfeit himself?" (Luke 9:25). It is important to remember that the money and things we accumulate come from and belong to God. We need to use them wisely, as He would, by sharing our resources with others and leading a simple lifestyle.

Spiritual Treasures for Reflection

"A good name is more desirable than great riches, and high esteem, than gold and silver." (Prov. 22:1)

"Honor the Lord with your wealth, with first fruits of all you produce. Then will your barns be filled with plenty, with new wine your vats will overflow." (Prov. 3:9–10)

"What profit is there for one to gain the whole world yet lose or forfeit himself?" (Luke 9:25)

Personal Notes of Reflection

_____

_____

_____

_____

_____

Chapter 8

Everyone Loses When Anger Rears Its Ugly Head

On December 1, 2016, former NFL player Joe McKnight and Ronald Gasser were involved in a road-rage incident. These two men were driving erratically in separate vehicles for about five miles, shouting vulgarities at each other along the way. They stopped their vehicles at a traffic intersection in a New Orleans suburb. Gasser acknowledged that he shot McKnight from his car as McKnight was standing at Gasser's passenger-side window. McKnight died as a result of the shooting, and Gasser was convicted of manslaughter. Anger reared its ugly head, resulting in a needless tragedy that will have long-lasting implications for everyone involved.

The emotion of anger is never a solution for a problem. This reaction only inflames an issue and either delays or prevents its resolution. Anger can lead to harmful wrath and evildoing. Psalms offer us great wisdom regarding anger. "Give up your anger; abandon your wrath; do not be provoked; it brings only harm" (Ps. 37:8).

All of us are subject to real-world situations that can open the door for the emotion of anger. Disputes between husbands and wives can lead to high levels of anger. Often, these disagreements result from simple matters such as cleaning duties or clothing choices. Also, anger can arise due to more serious matters, such as spending practices, work schedules, disciplining children, in-law issues, and marital misconduct. Other situations where this emotion can occur are in the workplace, at family gatherings, among neighbors, at recreational activities, and at sporting events.

Anger causes a wide range of behaviors. Raised voices are a common reaction. Some use a physical response to express their irritation, which can lead to abuse and injury. Family relationships, friendships, and job security are at risk when anger and abuse enter the situation. Nothing good happens when anger rears its ugly head.

Anger management can be a solution for this emotion. It can be accomplished by taking control of ourselves. "It is good sense in a man to be slow to anger, and it is his glory to overlook an offense" (Prov. 19:11).

The Mayo Clinic offers several tips to tame our tempers, which can be helpful:

- Take a timeout before responding to a challenging situation.
- Think before you respond because it is easy to say something you later regret.
- Gather your thoughts together before doing anything and allow others to do the same.
- Consider possible solutions that will solve the dispute rather than focusing on an angry response.
- After you have calmed down and collected your thoughts, offer your comments in a constructive way without hurting others.

- Never hold a grudge or negative feelings against someone who angered you; forgive, because an ongoing grudge has no value.[8]

Childcare is another situation where control of emotions is important. Parents, grandparents, and other family members face the challenges of the responsibility of raising or caring for children. When youngsters engage in misconduct, refuse to listen, and act irresponsibly, it is easy for caretakers to become exasperated. Just as we instruct children to go into timeout mode, we need to do the same to properly manage a situation. We want our children to conduct themselves appropriately, but we have to be reasonable about the process. St. Paul tells us that parents should not provoke their children so much that they become discouraged (Col. 3:21). Keep in mind that the response we make to the misconduct of our children will likely be imitated by them when they face the same situation later in life with their own youngsters.

Many times, when we are faced with stressful situations, the emotion of anger is riding right below the surface. Even the simplest of circumstances can provoke an eruption. These are the times when we must be calm in order to avoid an unnecessary, unproductive, negative, or harmful response. What is the point of robbing our joy by a slowly simmering anger? "Do not in spirit become quickly discontented, for discontent lodges in the bosom of a fool" (Eccles. 7:9).

Everyone should consider using life experiences as a foundation to develop self-control instincts. When I was fifteen years old and learning to play the game of golf, I would often get very

---

8 See "Anger Management: 10 Tips to Tame Your Temper," Mayo Clinic, February 29, 2020.

frustrated when my shots went awry. It was particularly frustrating for me when I would hit the ball into the water. My response as a teenager was to curse a few times and occasionally throw a golf club down the fairway.

One afternoon, I was playing golf with my father and a couple of his friends when my emotions got the best of me. After hitting a second ball into the water on the same hole, I threw the club I was using high into the air, and it almost got stuck in a tree. Judge John Boutall, who was playing with us that day, told me in a very kind way that it was time to grow up and stop this practice of venting my anger by tossing golf clubs. The comments by Judge Boutall were embarrassing because I realized what a fool I had been.

A few years ago, the billionaire investor Warren Buffet said, "It takes twenty years to build a reputation and five minutes to ruin it."[9] If you think about that statement, you'll do things differently. Anger outbursts can hurt our reputation. I remember my mother telling us to stay away from certain people because they had a bad temper. She was fearful that her sons would be hurt by these folks. As the Psalms tell us, anger brings only harm (Ps. 37:8). So if we value our reputation, we will do things differently. We can't let anger rear its ugly head.

Perhaps the simplest way to curb anger is to reflect on the words of the Prayer of St. Francis:

> Lord, make me an instrument of Your peace;
> where there is hatred, let me sow love;
> where there is injury, pardon;

---

[9]   "The Three Essential Warren Buffet Quotes to Live By," *Forbes*, April 20, 2014.

where there is doubt, faith;
where there is despair, hope;
where there is darkness, light;
where there is sadness, joy.

O divine Master, grant that I may not so much seek
to be consoled as to console,
to be understood as to understand,
to be loved as to love.
For it is in giving that we receive,
it is in pardoning that we are pardoned,
and it is in dying that we are born to eternal life.

Spiritual Treasures for Reflection

"Refrain from anger; abandon wrath; do not be provoked; it brings only harm." (Ps. 37:8)

"It is good sense in a man to be slow to anger, and it is his glory to overlook an offense." (Prov. 19:11)

"Do not in spirit become quickly discontented, for discontent lodges in the bosom of a fool." (Eccles. 7:9)

Personal Notes of Reflection

_____

_____

_____

_____

_____

Chapter 9

Self-Pride versus Humility: Coming Down from the Mountaintop

One of the most competitive events at the 2016 Summer Olympics was the 200-Meter Butterfly swimming race between Michael Phelps of the United States and Chad le Clos of South Africa. While in the locker room before the race, le Clos taunted Phelps by shadowboxing in front of him and staring him down. Phelps responded to these actions by humbly sitting in his chair without looking at his opponent. The South African swimmer continued exalting himself at the starting blocks by staring and waving at Phelps. Our U.S. swimmer refused to look in his competitor's direction and calmly focused on swimming the race. After the starting gun sounded, Phelps took the lead and easily won the race, earning the gold medal. His prideful competitor finished fourth without winning a medal. Michael Phelps, the humble swimmer, became the exalted winner. Chad le Clos, who had exalted himself, had to eat humble pie.

In Luke's Gospel, our Lord gives us His teaching on humility: "For everyone who exalts himself will be humbled, but the one who humbles himself will be exalted" (Luke 14:11). What does this word *humility* really mean? *Merriam-Webster* defines it as "freedom from pride or arrogance: the quality or state of being humble."

Jesus teaches us further about the message of humility in the parable about the invited guests and hosts at a wedding banquet:

> He told a parable to those who had been invited, noticing how they were choosing places of honor at the table. "When you are invited by someone to a wedding banquet, do not recline at table in the place of honor. A more distinguished guest than you may have been invited by him, and the host who invited both of you may approach you and say, 'Give your place to this man,' and then you would proceed with embarrassment to take the lowest place. Rather, when you are invited, go and take the lowest place so that when the host comes to you he may say, 'My friend, move up to a higher position.' Then you will enjoy the esteem of your companions at the table." (Luke 14:7–10)

From the Old Testament book of Sirach, the teacher, Ben Sirach, explains the importance of humility:

> My son, conduct your affairs with
> humility, and you will be loved more
>   than a giver of gifts.
> Humble yourself the more, the greater
> you are, and you will find favor with
>   God. (Sir. 3:17–18)

During our Lord's life on earth, He demonstrated humility repeatedly by the way He conducted himself. When baptized by His cousin John the Baptist, Jesus waited His turn at the back of the line like all the others, even though He was the Son of

God. At the Last Supper, Jesus washed the apostles' feet rather than being waited on. Also, our Lord freely accepted the most humiliating experience of earthly life. He was an alleged criminal with false charges levied against Him. He was convicted and sentenced to death for a crime He didn't commit. Jesus freely accepted the unjust, most humiliating form of death—public execution for all to see. Humility was a way of life for our Lord when He was on this earth.

Removing self-pride from our lives and replacing it with humility is a fundamental Christian value we all need to exemplify. It is hard to come down from the mountaintop. There are many ways we can demonstrate humility. For example, when at a social gathering, don't be the "hotshot" attention-grabber but rather be reserved and do not draw attention to yourself. Also, reach out to the least popular people in the room in order to make them feel like an important part of the group.

There are other times when we can show humility. When engaging in conversation with others, always talk about the interests of the other person and not your own. Simply stated, be selfless. When there is a line forming, take your place at the end. Don't cut in front of someone already standing there. Let others go before you. In the workplace, take an interest in the workers who are employed in all positions of the company to let them know that you truly have an interest in them. Don't just focus your attention on those who can be of help to you. In planning an event or party, don't give your hospitality just to the people who can repay you but include folks who you can't benefit from. If you are in the spotlight, deflect the attention away from yourself and praise others. Committing to this type of conduct is the essence of humility. The mountaintop of self-pride is no place for us to be.

Spiritual Excellence

The Queen of All Saints, Our Blessed Mother Mary, showed us the path to humility. She humbled herself to do the will of God, leaving behind her self-pride. Her sole focus was doing God's daily plan for her life. She said, "Behold, I am the handmaid of the Lord. May it be done to me according to your word" (Luke 1:38).

The Crescent City Classic is a ten-thousand-meter road race in New Orleans on Easter weekend. The first time our three sons, Blake, Kyle, and Grant, ran the race, they were all still in high school or college. Blake and Grant were avid runners and boasted of their potential finishes. They were talking about running fast times, finishing in the top five hundred of thirty thousand runners. Kyle was an athlete but also an offensive lineman on his high school football team at six feet, four inches tall and two hundred seventy pounds. His thoughts were geared toward just finishing the race. On race day, at mile five, Blake and Grant flamed out and were walking. Kyle quietly passed them by and finished the race ahead of them. That day, the humble brother came out on top.

In the race of life to reach the goal of Heaven, humility beats self-pride every time. Jesus always rewards the humble person. As our role model, our Lord was humble and void of self-pride.

Spiritual Treasures for Reflection

"My son, conduct your affairs with humility, and you will be loved more than a giver of gifts. Humble yourself the more, the greater you are, and you will find favor with God." (Sir. 3:17–18)

"For everyone who exalts himself will be humbled, but the one who humbles himself will be exalted." (Luke 14:11)

"Behold, I am the handmaid of the Lord. May it be done to me according to your word." (Luke 1:38)

Personal Notes of Reflection

_____

_____

_____

_____

_____

Chapter 10

The Challenge of Forgiving
Others Who Hurt Us

How do we respond when someone offends us? Through the Gospels, Jesus teaches us the process to follow when we are hurt by others.

In John's Gospel, we learn about Jesus teaching the people in the temple area. Some scribes and Pharisees brought a woman to Jesus who had been caught in adultery, and they made her stand in front of a crowd that had gathered. The scribes and Pharisees said to our Lord, "Now in the law, Moses commanded us to stone such women. So what do you say?" (John 8:5). These accusers were testing our Lord to see how He would answer their question. Initially, He responded by writing on the ground with His finger, as He probably sought guidance from the Holy Spirit. Then He said to the accusers, "Let the one among you who is without sin be the first to throw a stone at her" (John 8:7). The accusers were embarrassed and left. Jesus then showed forgiveness and mercy to the woman, saying, "Woman, where are they? Has no one condemned you?" Furthermore, He said, "Neither do I condemn you. Go, [and] from now on do not sin any more" (John 8:10, 11).

As Jesus taught us, the first step in the process of forgiving others who hurt us is to seek guidance from the Holy Spirit. The next step in the process is to have a dialogue with the wrongdoer to discuss the situation. Then we need to respond with forgiveness and mercy, not condemnation. Finally, we should help the offending party seek a fresh start.

On May 13, 1981, a tragic event happened in the world. A famous leader was shot four times with a semiautomatic pistol. Two bullets lodged in the victim's lower intestine while the other two injured his left index finger and right arm. This leader was rushed to the hospital for emergency surgery, and he survived the attack. The shooter was arrested, convicted, and sentenced to life imprisonment.

Two years after the shooting, the victim visited the attacker in prison and forgave him for his criminal act of attempted murder. The world leader I am referring to is Pope St. John Paul II. Not only did the pope forgive, but he asked the Italian government to pardon the attacker, and this request was honored. Pope St. John Paul II was truly Christ-like and a wonderful role model for us. He followed the process of forgiveness and mercy given to us by Jesus. After surviving the attempted murder, this great saint of our times most likely received guidance from the Holy Spirit as to how to respond to his attacker. He visited the shooter in prison, spoke to him, and forgave him. Then he helped the attacker get a fresh start through a pardon. This saint chose not to respond with the ordinary human emotions of hatred and vindictiveness.

There are life situations when we have a choice to make. We can forgive and show mercy to others, or we can retaliate against them for hurting us. For example, in everyday business activity, if someone intentionally takes advantage of us, the tendency is to want to punish them. Remember that expression, "I am going to teach him a lesson." Or what happens when someone says or does something that is hurtful toward our family? The natural tendency is to want to "make them pay for it." Also, when someone criticizes us directly or behind our back, how do we handle it? Do we carry a grudge and wait for the opportunity to respond in kind? Some people have been known to carry a grudge for years, waiting for a payback opportunity. By contrast, when one of our children's actions offend us, we should naturally respond with love, kindness, and forgiveness. Retaliation should never enter our minds. For instance, when a child spills a glass of milk on the floor, our response should be to clean up the mess and tell them to be more careful, not to yell at them. When our teenage son or daughter gets in his or her first accident, which costs us thousands of dollars, the best response is to encourage better driving practices and accountability for their actions. Likewise, in all situations in which we are victims of misconduct, our Lord teaches us not to retaliate but to respond with love, forgiveness, and mercy.

In Matthew's Gospel, the apostle Peter seeks understanding of our Lord's message of forgiveness. Peter asks, "Lord, if my brother sins against me, how often must I forgive him? As many as seven times?" Jesus answered, "I say to you, not seven times but seventy-seven times" (Matt. 18:21–22). Jesus further explained to Peter the depth of forgiveness expected in His parable of the unforgiving servant:

> That is why the kingdom of heaven may be likened to a king who decided to settle accounts with his servants. When he began the accounting, a debtor was brought before him who owed him a huge amount. Since he had no way of paying it back, his master ordered him to be sold,

along with his wife, his children, and all his property, in payment of the debt. At that, the servant fell down, did him homage, and said, "Be patient with me, and I will pay you back in full." Moved with compassion the master of that servant let him go and forgave him the loan. When that servant had left, he found one of his fellow servants who owed him a much smaller amount. He seized him and started to choke him, demanding, "Pay back what you owe." Falling to his knees, his fellow servant begged him, "Be patient with me, and I will pay you back." But he refused. Instead, he had him put in prison until he paid back the debt. Now when his fellow servants saw what had happened, they were deeply disturbed, and went to their master and reported the whole affair. His master summoned him and said to him, "You wicked servant! I forgave you your entire debt because you begged me to. Should you not have had pity on your fellow servant, as I had pity on you?" Then in anger his master handed him over to the torturers until he should pay back the whole debt. So will my heavenly Father do to you, unless each of you forgives his brother from his heart. (Matt. 18:23–35)

This issue is so important that our Lord even put His message of forgiveness in the prayer He taught us to say to God, our Father. The Lord's Prayer states in this pertinent part, "Our Father in heaven, hallowed be your name.... Forgive us our debts, as we forgive our debtors" (Matt. 6:9, 12). In Matthew's Gospel, our Lord is very direct when He says, "If you forgive others their transgressions, your heavenly Father will forgive you. But if you do not forgive others, neither will your Father forgive your transgressions" (Matt. 6:14–15).

Jesus further emphasized forgiveness in His Sermon on the Mount when He gave us this beatitude: "Blessed are the merciful, for they will be shown mercy" (Matt. 5:7). Jesus expressly tells us that by being merciful and forgiving others, we will get the benefit of His mercy for our acts of misconduct.

Jesus practiced what He preached on the issue of forgiveness. When He was wrongly sentenced to death, tortured, and crucified, He never once resented, hated, or retaliated. His response was just the opposite. He demonstrated great mercy and love by asking God to forgive His torturers and executioners.

The natural human response when we are hurt by others is to become emotional. We can become angry, judgmental, resentful, and retaliatory. Jesus tells us that there is no place for these human emotions. He is looking to us for a spiritual response, and He taught us a process to follow when these situations arise. The first step is to pause, be calm, and seek guidance from the Holy Spirit. Then we should have a dialogue with the wrongdoer to discuss the situation. The next step is to show mercy and forgiveness. Finally, we should help the one who hurt us.

Take the high road and turn a negative into a positive. After all, our Lord will show us mercy for our trespasses against those we offended.

Spiritual Treasures for Reflection

"Let the one among you who is without sin be the first to throw a stone at her." (John 8:7)

" 'Lord, if my brother sins against me, how often must I forgive him? As many as seven times?' Jesus answered, 'I say to you, not seven times but seventy-seven times.' " (Matt. 18:21–22)

"If you forgive others their transgressions, your heavenly Father will forgive you. But if you do not forgive others, neither will your Father forgive your transgressions." (Matt. 6:14–15)

Personal Notes of Reflection

_____

_____

_____

_____

_____

Chapter 11

Overcoming Selfishness: Become a Spiritual Winner for Jesus by Serving Others

Americans love a winner. It has always been that way. We love our Olympic champions such as Michael Phelps, Simone Biles, and Carl Lewis. Local communities have great passion for their sports teams to win championships. This includes professional teams such as the New Orleans Saints, the Chicago Cubs, or the Golden State Warriors and college teams such as the Alabama Crimson Tide, the Ohio State Buckeyes, and the Texas Longhorns. Americans love a winner so much that they even bet money on their sports teams to win. Some fans take their team support to a higher level. They dress up in costumes, paint their faces, make funny signs, and cheer wildly. Many wear a jersey that represents one of the stars of their favorite team. In the Bible, Jesus teaches us how to be a winner in our spiritual life. He says that we can't be selfish. We have to be *selfless*, acting as a servant to those around us.

In Mark's Gospel, the apostles James and John tell Jesus that they want to sit next to Him in Heaven, one on His right and the other on His left. The request by these two apostles is clearly selfish. They put themselves ahead of the other ten apostles, prophets such as Elijah, Jeremiah, Isaiah, and the saints. James and John demonstrate their egos and selfish desires in their request to our Lord. In this Gospel passage, the other ten apostles react to the request by being indignant toward James and John. Perhaps some of these apostles thought that they deserved to sit next to Jesus. In response to the selfish statements of James and John and the resentment of the other ten apostles, Jesus said, "Whoever wishes to be great among you will be your servant; whoever wishes to be first among you will be the slave of all" (Mark 10:43–44).

Our Lord showed us how to be a spiritual winner by His selfless nature. In His public life, He left His family home, lived in poverty, and relied on the generosity of strangers for food and a place to sleep at night. He owned nothing other than the clothes on His back. Jesus was a true servant to all.

Serving others by teaching God's ways was His constant mission. He preached to them through parables and straight talk, performed miracles, cast out demons, and raised the dead. Jesus taught us how to pray to God His Father by teaching us the Lord's Prayer. Our Lord did nothing for Himself and put all His power, wisdom, energy, and talents to work for us. Ultimately, He gave up His life for us, freely accepting His fate of cruel torture and execution. He gave His life as ransom for all souls.

Selflessness and service to others are achievable by each of us. Parents do this naturally by bringing children into the world, devoting time to their upbringing, and providing them an education in order to give them the best possible start in life. Workers can be selfless when they earn income for the family, add value to the company performance, and pursue perfection in their jobs.

Managers serve others by treating those they manage with respect and dignity and leading others by example. Ministries such as the Knights of Columbus, meals for the homeless, and Eucharistic minister visits to the homebound offer service opportunities. People with an active prayer life are selfless by praying for the needs of family members, friends, and others.

Overcoming selfishness means to love others. St. Paul tells us about love in his First Letter to the Corinthians. He says, "Love is patient, love is kind. It is not jealous, love is not pompous, it is not inflated, it is not rude, it does not seek its own interests, it is not quick-tempered, it does not brood over injury.... It bears all things, believes all things, hopes all things, endures all things" (1 Cor. 13:4, 5, 7). Furthermore, in his Letter to the Philippians, he states, "Do nothing out of selfishness or out of vainglory; rather, humbly regard others as more important than yourselves" (Phil. 2:3). Finally, St. Paul tells us in his Letter to the Romans, "Let each of us please our neighbor for the good, for building up" (Rom. 15:2). Likewise, it is important to know that selfish behavior can lead to misconduct. "For where jealousy and selfish ambition exist, there is disorder and every foul practice" (James 3:16).

The saints are spiritual winners and can be role models for us. One of them is St. Vincent de Paul, who was ordained a priest in 1600. While in Rome, he became a chaplain to the Count of Goigny and had the duty of distributing money to the deserving poor. Thereafter, he spent his life in service to the poor by providing relief, preaching missions, and establishing hospitals for their care. He founded the religious order Congregation of the Mission, also known as the Vincentians, to carry out his work. St. Vincent de Paul dedicated his life to serving others. His efforts led to the formation of the St. Vincent de Paul Society, which is a ministry dedicated to taking care of the poor. St Vincent de Paul led a life of selflessness.

Our daughter-in-law Ashley Eason teaches pre-K students at an elementary school in Springdale, Arkansas. At the end of the 2018 school year, one of her four-year-old students was abandoned by her parents. Ashley and our son Blake made the decision to take the student into their home and apply to be foster parents. At the end of the summer, the student returned home to live with her mother. Accepting the abandoned student into their home was a wonderful, selfless act.

Think about it this way. Sometimes, we can get so caught up in what we want for ourselves that our motto becomes: "My will be done." Of course, Jesus taught us the opposite in His prayer to His Father. Our Lord's motto was: "Thy will be done." Replacing the word "my" with the word "Thy" will help us change the focus from ourselves to our Lord.

Winning championships brings earthly acclaim. But every day is an opportunity to be a spiritual winner in the eyes of Jesus by serving others and not ourselves. As Jesus said, "Whoever wishes to be great among you will be your servant; whoever wishes to be first among you will be the slave of all" (Mark 10:43–44).

Spiritual Treasures for Reflection

"Do nothing out of selfishness or out of vainglory; rather, humbly regard others as more important than yourselves." (Phil. 2:3)

"For where jealousy and selfish ambition exist, there is disorder and every foul practice." (James 3:16)

"Whoever wishes to be great among you will be your servant; whoever wishes to be first among you will be the slave of all." (Mark 10:43–44)

Personal Notes of Reflection

_____

_____

_____

_____

_____

Chapter 12

Spiritual Time Management: Is Our Lord in Last Place in My Life?

It's 6:15 a.m., and the alarm goes off. You jump up out of bed, take a shower, dress, and rush through a morning meal consisting of a breakfast bar chased by a caffeine drink. Then you jump in the car and drive through traffic, including seemingly endless road construction. At work, you crank through the morning, which is filled with meetings, appointments, phone conferences, and email responses. At lunchtime, you wolf down a sandwich. The afternoon is spent in a blur similar to your morning. After work, you race home and put something in the microwave that will fill your stomach. Homework with your children and some light housework round out the evening. About to collapse, you entertain yourself through television, the internet, or social media. A quick prayer ends your day, and you fall asleep for an inadequate amount of time. The next day you, wake up tired but jump right back into the same pattern. Does this seem familiar?

Wow! What is missing from this lifestyle? There is little to no place for our Lord. He has taken a backseat to everything else. We must reverse the order to make Jesus first in our lives, because He has the keys to eternal life. In John's Gospel, we are told that the Son of Man must "be lifted up" (John 3:14).

Spiritual Excellence

The crucifix is set in a high place in nearly every corner of the world: churches, chapels, homes, classrooms, and hospitals. The crucifix is elevated even on mountaintops, such as in Rio de Janeiro, Brazil; Mount Samat, Philippines; and Caraiman Peak, Romania. We, too, must elevate Jesus to be our top priority. He cannot be a Sunday-only God.

With all that Jesus was tasked with accomplishing during His short time on earth, He practiced spiritual time management. He regularly left the apostles and disciples to pray to His Father. He was seeking guidance and direction from God. His prayer time kept Him focused on God's plan and prevented Him from succumbing to earthly temptations from the evil one. "In those days He departed to the mountain to pray, and He spent the night in prayer to God" (Luke 6:12). Furthermore, we read, "Rising very early before dawn, he left and went off to a deserted place, where He prayed" (Mark 1:35). And Matthew's Gospel says, "After doing so, he went up on the mountain by himself to pray. When it was evening he was there alone" (Matt. 14:23).

How do we spend our free time? Often, we spend time entertaining ourselves by watching television or movies, surfing the internet, listening to music, reading the paper, emailing, texting, or tweeting. We fill our time learning about people, ideas, and news that will be unimportant or forgotten tomorrow. Does anyone remember once-popular celebrities such as Gloria Swanson, the Dorsey Brothers, or Red Grange? By contrast, our Lord Jesus lived two thousand years ago, yet He is here today and always will be. We fill up our free time with media or meaningless activities but spend little to no time with Jesus. We turn our back on the One who should be the center of our lives.

There can be adverse side effects from overexposure to the media. Temptations of all kinds can flourish and control us. Many television shows and movies have immoral scenes or innuendos. Some segments of the internet promote pornography. Greed for money and power can consume us and create jealous hearts. Then there is gossip and trash talk on social media that hurts the reputation of friends, neighbors, or co-workers. For some users of social media, bullying has become a way of life, whether they be aggressors or unfortunate victims.

Video games often consume the time of our teenagers to the exclusion of productive activities. Also, there are television shows that seem to glorify criminal misconduct. Do we really have to respond to every text or email each day while ignoring quality prayer time? Consider fasting from select media activities to spend time with Jesus, His Mother Mary, and the saints.

How should we respond to the call in John's Gospel to make Jesus our top priority? We can start by adding some spiritual time management to our day. Through her apparitions in places such as Fátima, Portugal; Guadalupe, Mexico; and Lourdes, France, Our Blessed Mother Mary tells us that we must pray frequently.

Consider this spiritual time management plan. Upon awakening in the morning, pray for guidance from the Holy Spirit to do the will of God, including in specific actions you will be involved with during the day. On the drive to work or carpool, rather than listening to the radio, pray for the souls in Purgatory, especially for family members and friends who may need your help. At lunchtime, reflect on the morning activities and plan for the afternoon with guidance from the Holy Spirit. After lunch, spend five to ten minutes praying a decade of the Rosary. On the drive home, examine your conscience as to how you conducted yourself that day, consider whether you worked for the Lord, doing His will, or fell short in some way, and thank Him for the many blessings He bestowed on you. Pray with your family at dinner.

Finally, at the end of the day, spend five to ten minutes in spiritual reading before falling asleep. Scripture, a book about the saints, or spiritual inspirational books are good selections. Putting spiritual thoughts in your mind at the end of the day will give you a wonderful night of peaceful rest. Keep in mind that our Blessed Mother Mary, in her many apparitions all over the world, calls us to frequent prayer during the day to obtain spiritual guidance. There are numerous ideas to consider when developing your personal spiritual time management plan. A plan that is focused on our Lord through a daily regimen is key to a successful one.

We can learn from those who have gone before us. Remember the story of the Magi? Jesus was such a top priority that shortly after His birth, they traveled from their faraway home to see Him. He was the Messiah. In ancient times, travel involved risk from outlaws, wild animals, and harsh weather. These wise men and kings so loved Jesus that they gave Him their treasures of gold, frankincense, and myrrh. They visited with Mary and Joseph and spent adoration time with Jesus (Matt. 2:1–12). In our world today, we don't have to travel hundreds of miles to be with Jesus. All we have to do is simply invite Him into our hearts each day. Our souls naturally desire a relationship with our Lord daily as a top priority. We have an innate thirst for Jesus if we don't block out this desire with our free will. We cannot let our free will get in the way of the natural inclination of our souls.

Through our church ministry, we bring the Holy Eucharist to nursing home residents in New Orleans, many of whom have Alzheimer's disease or advanced dementia. One of the patients, Miss Ethel, could not communicate well and was bedridden. Despite these various ailments, her soul knew the way to our Lord. When we prayed the Lord's Prayer with her, she was able to recite it. She was speaking with her soul. It was her only verbal communication.

A deacon friend passed away after suffering with Alzheimer's disease. In his last days, he was unable to communicate even with his family, yet he knew simple prayers. When given the Eucharist, he would say: "I want to be with Jesus forever." Our Lord was the top priority for this deacon.

So spend some quality quiet time developing your plan for daily spiritual time management. Consider these questions in developing your plan:

- Is our Lord truly number one in my life?
- Do I pray frequently as requested by Our Blessed Mother during her apparitions?
- Am I blocking my soul's desire for Jesus with excessive self-entertainment through the overuse of media and other activities?

Spiritual Treasures for Reflection

The Son of Man must be lifted up. (see John 3:14)

Jesus "departed to the mountain to pray, and he spent the night in prayer" to God. (Luke 6:12)

Personal Notes of Reflection

_____

_____

_____

_____

_____

Chapter 13

Working on My 401(s) Plan
for Eternal Retirement

Companies regularly advertise their skill and experience at providing us with wonderful 401(k) retirement plans to achieve financial independence and live well in our later years. As many of the promotions indicate, a well-heeled 401(k) plan gives the retiree an ideal earthly life, living in sunny Florida or Arizona, taking trips around the world, doing various recreational activities and residing in a nice home without a care in the world. However, the acquisition of money and earthly things doesn't do anything for our eternal retirement.

We need to be working daily on our "401(s)" spirituality plan for our eternal retirement, utilizing our spiritual talents for our Lord. The 401(s) plan is our spiritual bank account. The 401(k) plan is only good for a very limited time during this earthly life, whereas the 401(s) plan is good for eternity.

Our Lord uses a parable to explain the importance of utilizing our spiritual talents to build up our 401(s) plan. In Matthew's Gospel, Jesus tells His disciples the familiar parable of the talents. In this parable, a man preparing for a journey called three of his workers together. He gave each of them some talents with the expectation that they would fully utilize them to add value to his fortune while he was away. To one, he gave five talents. To another, two. And to a third, one talent. Two of the three workers maximized their efforts, thereby doubling the return on their talents for the owner. The third worker buried the one talent he was given in the ground, thereby doing nothing with it (Matt. 25:14–18).

Upon his return, the owner settled accounts with the three workers. The two workers who maximized their talents were rewarded with greater responsibilities and shared in the owner's joy. As to the third worker, the owner gave him a very harsh response: "You wicked, lazy servant! ... Should you not then have put my money in the bank so that I could have got it back with interest on my return? ... Throw this useless servant into the darkness outside, where there will be wailing and grinding of teeth" (Matt. 25:26, 27, 30).

Why does our Lord give us this message? You see, He has great expectations for each one of us to do His will, and He has put us here for a specific purpose. Our Lord expects us to make a difference in the world for Him, adding value to all those around us. Jesus asks us to be selfless, always doing for others.

Our Lord gives us some guidelines to follow in fulfilling His spiritual plan for us. Adversity cannot distract us from our mission for Him. We can't reach our potential if we are sitting on the sidelines of life, acting as though the talents he gave us are buried in the ground. Do not be jealous of another's talents, because all that counts is that we use the talents that we are given. Each one of us is on a personal mission for Our Savior, and our performance matters for others.

We only have a finite amount of time to maximize our talents. That could be a day, a month, or many years. St. Paul tells us in his First Letter to the Thessalonians that our end to this life may come like a thief in the night, when we least expect it (1 Thess. 5:2). Consequently, we need to maximize our spiritual talents while we still have time.

How do we make use of our spiritual talents? All of us are at a different stage in our lives. It is important that we maximize these talents at each stage. As students, we need to behave in class, make the best grades that we can, and help our parents, brothers, and sisters. As workers, it is important that we strive to help the company by our efforts and support our co-workers. For parents, we need to always be there for our children, discipline them as needed, and be a role model at all times. Retirement isn't the time to simply ride off into the sunset and think only about ourselves. Rather, this is the time to get closer to our Lord and give back to Him for all He has blessed us with in our lifetime. It is a time to consider being a volunteer, because our Church and community need us.

Unfortunately, we sometimes fall short of our Lord's expectations. Each day, we have one of three choices to make. One choice is to simply be lazy, underperform, and be self-indulgent. Another is to be mediocre or average, just getting by. The third one is to maximize our spiritual talents by being an overachiever in doing our Lord's will. Based on Jesus' parable of the talents, it is crystal clear that the third choice is not an option: it is the *only* path to follow.

On September 25, 2006, in the Louisiana Superdome, the New Orleans Saints were playing the Atlanta Falcons in the first game in the dome stadium after Hurricane Katrina. An undrafted free agent, who was five feet, eleven inches tall and weighed two hundred pounds, became a hero that night. Steve Gleason blocked a punt by the Falcons that ignited the Saints to victory and helped give the City of New Orleans a rebirth following the devastation from the hurricane.

Gleason maximized his talents as a special team player, inspiring us all. Sadly, in 2011, Gleason contracted amyotrophic lateral sclerosis (ALS), which completely changed his life. Rather than going into hiding and becoming a recluse, he has spent his time raising money for research and support for ALS patients. This former professional football player, now ALS patient, continues to maximize his talents despite a serious disease that has compromised his life. Gleason has exercised the third option of maximizing his talents despite the harshest of circumstances.

Why is it important to take our Lord's message seriously? The answer is simple: Our eternal destiny depends upon it. At the end of our lives, each one of us will face Jesus one-on-one to account for the talents that He had given us. What will our response be to the question, "What did you do with the talents I gave you to make the earthly world a better place?" We can't spin our response, nor can we give half-truths. He already knows the answer to the question. The spotlight will be on each one of us at that time. We will have to account for our time during our earthly life.

What will our Lord say to our response to His question? Will it be, "Well done, my good and faithful servant ... Come, share your master's joy" (Matt. 25:23)? Or will it be, "You wicked, lazy servant! ... Throw this useless servant into the darkness outside, where there will be wailing and grinding of teeth" (Matt. 25:26, 30)?

St. Mother Teresa of Calcutta, India, described the issue this way in these verses from her prayer, "Do it Anyway":

> The good you do today, will often be forgotten.
> Do good anyway.
> Give the best you have, and it will never be
> enough. Give your best anyway.

In the final analysis, it is between you and God.
It was never between you and them anyway.
(The Prayer Foundation)

We spend so much time during our work lives building up our 401(k) plan for an earthly retirement. What are we doing to build up our 401(s) plan for eternity? Remember, this plan is our spiritual bank account. It is far more important than our 401(k) account. We should make certain our 401(s) plan has enough in it to provide for a wonderful, eternal retirement.

Spiritual Treasures for Reflection

"For you yourselves know very well that the day of the Lord will come like a thief at night." (1 Thess. 5:2)

"Well done, my good and faithful servant.... Come, share your master's joy." (Matt. 25:23)

"You wicked lazy servant!... Should you not then have put my money in the bank so that I could have got it back with interest on my return?... Throw this useless servant into the darkness outside, where there will be wailing and grinding of teeth." (Matt. 25:26, 30)

Personal Notes of Reflection

_____

_____

_____

_____

_____

Part III

Remedies to Restore Our Souls to a Natural State of Happiness and Holiness and Lead Us to Heaven

Chapter 14

Learning to Pursue Spiritual Excellence

One of the most famous football coaches in America is Lou Holtz. Perhaps he is known best for his 1988 National Championship Notre Dame football team. The team finished the season undefeated with a perfect 12-0 record. Holtz, a devout Catholic, retired from coaching and has become an author and well-known speaker. One of his books is titled *Winning Every Day: The Game Plan for Success.* In the book, Holtz describes ten steps for his game plan for success. One of them is to commit to excellence. He states, "Do everything to the best of your ability. Everybody wants to be associated with people who set and maintain high standards. When you lower standards, you only invite mediocrity."

Excellence is a term often discussed not just in sports but in many areas of life, including education, business, and healthcare. In education, students are encouraged by their teachers and parents to develop good work habits in order to excel in the classroom and on standardized tests, resulting in opportunities for success. Business owners and managers ask their employees to do their best in the workplace in order to achieve personal success and growth of the business. Physicians and nurses are dedicated to providing excellent care to their patients in order to give them the best quality of life.

Spiritual Excellence

The twentieth-century historian Will Durant summarized Aristotle's teachings on excellence in this way: "Excellence is an art won by training and habituation. We do not act rightly because we have virtue or excellence, but we rather have those because we have acted rightly. We are what we repeatedly do. Excellence, then, is not an act but a habit."[10]

In our faith, we seldom hear about the concept of pursuing spiritual excellence. Yet it is the path to happiness, holiness, and Heaven. Scripture provides us with several references on the topic of spiritual excellence. The apostle St. Paul tells us, "Finally, brothers, whatever is true, whatever is honorable, whatever is just, whatever is pure, whatever is lovely, whatever is gracious, if there is any excellence and if there is anything worthy of praise, think about these things" (Phil. 4:8). St. Paul further speaks about spiritual excellence in his Letter to the Colossians, "Whatever you do, do from the heart, as for the Lord and not for others, knowing that you will receive from the Lord the due payment of the inheritance; be slaves of the Lord Christ" (Col. 3:23–24). Also, St. Paul states, "Now as you excel in every respect, in faith, discourse, knowledge, all earnestness, and in the love we have for you, may you excel in this gracious act also" (2 Cor. 8:7).

Jesus, as our teacher, instructs us about spiritual excellence. He tells us that He is the Way, the Truth, and the Life and that no one can reach His Father except through Him (John 14:6). To follow our Lord's ways, we must adopt His will in place of our own will. To pursue spiritual excellence means we must subordinate our will in favor of our Lord's will in all that we do each day.

In simple terms, spiritual excellence means always to do God's will. Remember that our Lord taught His apostles this spiritual

[10] Forbes Quotes, Forbes.com.

message when He told them how to pray. "This is how you are to pray: Our Father in heaven, hallowed be your name, your kingdom come, your will be done, on earth as in heaven" (Matt. 6:8–10).

So how are we going to lead a life dedicated to pursuing spiritual excellence? We have to make good choices each day to do God's will. We have to listen to the voice of the Good Shepherd and not the evil one. In John's Gospel, Jesus tells us the parable of the good shepherd. In the story, there are competing voices for the care of the sheep. The voice of the thief or evildoer attempts to guide the sheep with the goal of stealing and slaughtering them. The other voice is that of Jesus, the Good Shepherd. He is engaged in an intense battle for the sheep because He loves them, and they belong to Him. He desperately wants His sheep to follow His message so that they might have life and may have it more abundantly. Jesus calls each of His sheep by name. Our Lord tells us that whoever follows His direction will be saved and find pasture. So we have to listen to the voice of our Good Shepherd in doing His will and not to the voice of the evil one (John 10:1–10).

There is a spiritual battle raging in the world today among these voices competing for our souls. The thief is attempting to influence us by bombarding us with all kinds of enticements to join his team, to steer us away from God's will so we will pursue spiritual decadence. He uses various types of temptations to exploit our weaknesses, such as alcohol consumption, material things, jealousy, pornography, improper television and social media usage, illegal-drug use, and fake news. The evildoer wants us to become dependent on these earthly things and on his ways.

By contrast, Jesus our Good Shepherd is constantly reaching out to us so that we will recognize His message and become dependent on Him. He does this through the sacraments of Holy

Eucharist, Confession, and daily Mass. Paying the Rosary to our Blessed Mother Mary and studying Scripture and the exemplary lives of the saints can guide us. Additionally, participation in parish ministry opportunities to serve others may bring us closer to Jesus.

This battle among competing voices for our souls to choose between spiritual excellence and spiritual decadence has been occurring since the time of Adam and Eve. Choose spiritual excellence. Remember, Adam and Eve had the choice whether to eat the forbidden fruit. The evil one convinced them to make a decision against God's will (Gen. 3:1–13).

In pursuing spiritual excellence, each one of us has a choice to make as to which voice we are going to follow. Is it going to be the Good Shepherd's or the thief's? We see this challenge in our daily actions. For example, when we go to the shopping mall to look for a new suit or dress and find it, a thought may enter our mind. New shoes would look great with this suit or dress. But the Good Shepherd has a different opinion. You don't need those shoes. Save the money for a family need and don't spend it on yourself.

Other examples include consuming one more alcoholic drink and overlooking your responsibility to drive home. The evil one tempts you to have that drink, whereas the Good Shepherd tells you that it's time to stop, as you have to drive yourself and/or others home safely. In another situation, you are faced with the choice to fire a new employee who made a mistake during the early days of his employment. The evil one tempts you to terminate him to demonstrate your superiority over others. But the Good Shepherd instructs you to give the employee a second chance.

Fr. John Riccardo recently authored a book entitled *Heaven Starts Now: Becoming a Saint Day by Day.*[11] He specifically dis-

---

[11] The Word Among Us Press, 2016.

cusses the importance of listening to the voice of our Lord. He states, "When my heart is engaged with the Lord, I'm really listening to Him, and I'm pouring out what's going on in my life. If I don't regularly, daily, persistently, and intentionally strive to listen to the Lord about everything in my life, it is no wonder that when I have a big decision and go to Him, I have a hard time hearing Him. I have not accustomed my ears to hear His voice."

Fortunately, we have many great role models to follow who chose a path to pursue spiritual excellence. Our Blessed Mother Mary made a choice to be subservient to the will of God at all times. She began this journey when she freely accepted the call from God to be the Mother of Our Savior. Later in her life, when her Son, Jesus, was falsely accused, prosecuted, and crucified, she didn't interfere, because she knew that these things had to happen. How hard was it for her to be obedient to the will of God without trying to save her Son?

All the saints followed the call to obedience to God as well. Let us revisit the words St. Thérèse of Lisieux wrote in her autobiography: "My God, I choose all. I don't want to be a saint by halves. I'm not afraid to suffer for You, I fear only one thing: to keep my own will. So take it, for I choose all that You will."[12]

So what are the benefits of leading a life by doing the will of Jesus? We will experience great happiness and holiness as well as courage and strength to handle our most challenging times. To choose a life of spiritual decadence that is filled with stress, anxiety, and worry makes no sense. Ultimately, making the correct choice to pursue spiritual excellence by doing the will of God will lead us to Heaven.

---

[12] *Story of a Soul*, 27.

Spiritual Treasures for Reflection

"Finally, brothers, whatever is true, whatever is honorable, whatever is just, whatever is pure, whatever is lovely, whatever is gracious, if there is any excellence and if there is anything worthy of praise, think about these things." (Phil. 4:8)

"Now as you excel in every respect, in faith, discourse, knowledge, all earnestness, and in the love we have for you, may you excel in this gracious act also." (2 Cor. 8:7)

"If I don't regularly, daily, persistently, and intentionally strive to listen to the Lord about everything in my life, it is no wonder that when I have a big decision and go to Him, I have a hard time hearing Him. I have not accustomed my ears to hear His voice." (Fr. John Riccardo)

"My God, I choose all. I don't want to be a saint by halves. I'm not afraid to suffer for You, I fear only one thing: to keep my own will. So take it, for I choose all that You will." (St. Thérèse of Lisieux)

Personal Notes of Reflection

_____

_____

_____

_____

_____

Chapter 15

The Holy Spirit: Putting the Greatest Power on Earth to Work within Us

When we think of great power, we often contemplate political strength, athletic skills, business prowess, or intellectual abilities. The vast majority of us will never experience these kinds of powers. However, the undeniable truth in this life is that these earthly powers are only temporary and pale by comparison to the supernatural power of the Holy Spirit. The power of the Holy Spirit is available to each of us, not just to a select few.

Scripture tells us about the power of the Holy Spirit:

Now to him who is able to accomplish far more than all we ask or imagine, by the power at work within us. (Eph. 3:20)

For God did not give us a spirit of cowardice but rather of power and love and self-control. (2 Tim. 1:7)

I have the strength for everything through him who empowers me. (Phil. 4:13)

But you will receive power when the holy spirit comes upon you, and you will be my witnesses in Jerusalem, throughout Judea and Samaria, and to the ends of the earth. (Acts 1:8)

I will put my spirit within you and make you live by my statutes, careful to observe my decrees. (Ezek. 36:27)

This supernatural power from the Holy Spirit was given to the apostles three days after Jesus was crucified. The apostles were locked in the upper room, afraid that they would be crucified just like our Lord. Jesus appeared to them and told them twice, "Peace be with you" (John 20:19; 20:21). Our Lord then breathed on them and said, "Receive the Holy Spirit" (John 20:22). Our Lord even more strikingly poured out the Holy Spirit on the apostles at Pentecost (Acts 2:1–4; CCC 1287, 1556). Blessed with the power of the Holy Spirit, the apostles, simple fishermen and laborers, were able to overcome all their fears, worries, and anxieties. These founders of the Church performed miracles and served the poor. All but one of them was crucified for their beliefs.

Throughout the books of the New Testament, diaries of the saints, encyclicals of the popes, and writings of many believers, many have professed the great power of the Holy Spirit at work in their lives. The Holy Spirit has healed countless physical, emotional, and spiritual ills, cured seemingly endless addictions, solved immeasurable personal, family, friend and work-related problems, and given peace to the fearful and anxious. In the history of the Church, there have been thousands of martyrs who died for their faith. They were able to handle their great suffering and death through the power of the Holy Spirit.

Testimony to the power of the Holy Spirit can be found in the stoning martyrdom of one of the first deacons of the Church, St. Stephen. Filled with the Holy Spirit, St. Stephen was performing great wonders and signs among the people and preaching to them. Many people disagreed with his spiritual message, and he was arrested, charged with blasphemy, and brought before the Sanhedrin. During his trial, St. Stephen defended his position, which angered the Sanhedrin. In response to their anger, he was filled with the Holy Spirit and looked up to Heaven and said, "Behold, I see the heavens opened and the Son of Man standing at the right hand of God" (Acts 7:56). After hearing this, they threw him out of the city and began to stone him. As they were stoning St. Stephen, he called out, "Lord Jesus, receive my spirit" (Acts 7:59).

The Holy Spirit offers us powerful gifts and fruits. The gifts are wisdom, understanding, counsel, fortitude, knowledge, piety, and fear of our Lord (see Isa. 11:2). The fruits of the Holy Spirit are love, joy, peace, patience, kindness, generosity, faithfulness, gentleness, and self-control (Gal. 5:22–23). All these gifts and fruits are available to us through the power of the Holy Spirit.

Do you remember the history of the apostle Peter, the fisherman? Before he received the gifts and fruits of the Holy Spirit, he had a strong personality and often acted impulsively. Remember, he doubted Jesus, sank in the water, cut off the ear of a soldier, and denied Jesus three times. After receiving the great gifts and fruits of the Holy Spirit at Pentecost, St. Peter became the rock upon which the early Church was built. He converted from denying Jesus to being a leader in spreading the good news of our Lord. As a result of his evangelization efforts for the early Church, he was crucified upside down.

Can the decision to allow the Holy Spirit to drive our lives really make a big difference? Absolutely! We spend so much of our time trying to do things on our own that we let self-pride and selfishness control us. Frequently, we think to ourselves, "I can do this on my own. I don't need anybody's help." This thought process often leads to sinfulness, poor decision-making, and un-happiness. By following this pride-driven philosophy of life, we are missing out on the gifts and fruits of the Holy Spirit that can make our lives a thousand times better. Why would anyone choose a life of unhappiness, poor decision-making, anger, and selfishness that comes with prideful self-direction? It is immea-surably better to pursue a life filled with guidance from the Holy Spirit through the gifts of wisdom, understanding, courage, and knowledge and the fruits of joy, peace, patience, and self-control.

If we accept them, the gifts and fruits of the Holy Spirit will help us with major decisions and daily activities. The gifts of wisdom, understanding, and knowledge will guide us in major decisions such as career choices, education selections for our children, medical dilemmas, and financial or business decisions. These same gifts will guide us in daily circumstances, such as time management, work-related issues, social matters, childrearing, and our spiritual life.

How do we put the power of the Holy Spirit to work for us? The simple answer is frequent prayer during the day with our Lord and Savior. Developing a relationship with Jesus and the Holy Spirit is similar to a relationship one has with a spouse, sibling, or best friend. Much like we spend quality time each day with these loved ones, we need to spend quality prayer time with Jesus and the Holy Spirit.

Prayer time is easy to accomplish if you think about it. Let us review: In the morning, pray for guidance from the Holy Spirit to do the will of God, in all the actions you will be involved in during the day. On the drive to work or carpool, rather than lis-tening to the radio, pray for the souls in Purgatory, especially for family members and friends who may need our help. At lunch-time, reflect on the morning activities and plan for the afternoon with guidance from the Holy Spirit. After lunch, spend five to ten minutes praying a decade of the Rosary. On the drive home, examine your conscience as to how you conducted yourself that day, consider whether you worked for the Lord, doing His will, or fell short in some way, and thank Him for the many blessings He bestowed upon you. Pray with your family at dinner. Finally, at the end of the day, spend five to ten minutes in spiritual reading before falling asleep. The Bible, a book about the saints, or spiritual inspirational books are good selections. Putting spiritual thoughts in your mind at the end of the day will give you a wonderful night of peaceful rest. Keep in mind that our Blessed Mother Mary, in her many apparitions all over the world, calls us to frequent prayer during the day to obtain divine spiritual guidance.

Devote time to daily prayer in order to reap the rewards of the powerful gifts and fruits of the Holy Spirit. After all, a major reason Jesus came to earth was to ignite the power of the Holy Spirit in the apostles, and in all of us, in order to give us guidance and direction to be in total communion with Him. With the Holy Spirit at work in us, we will have an abundantly happy and joyous life and clear guidance in all our actions each day. It is critical that we permit the Holy Spirit to be the automated driver of our souls for all our decisions and actions each day. As St. Paul said,

> But when the kindness and generous love
> of God our savior appeared,
> not because of any righteous deeds we had done
> but because of His mercy,
> he saved us through the bath of rebirth
> and renewal of the holy Spirit,
> whom He richly poured out on us
> through Jesus Christ our Savior. (Titus 3:4–6)

Spiritual Excellence

In my early thirties, my life was in a constant state of turmoil. My father was in poor health, we had three little boys to raise, and I was overwhelmed by my law practice. Peace, joy, and happiness were absent from my life. It was time to put the great power of the Holy Spirit to work, so I turned to Jesus for help. I began to pray frequently during the day and read the Bible. Our Lord responded by putting the wonderful gifts and fruits of the Holy Spirit to work in me. By changing my prayer life, reading the Bible, and developing a relationship with Jesus, my life was transformed forever. Our Lord has truly blessed me and my family all these years through the great power of the Holy Spirit.

Please don't let another day go by with your life filled with turmoil and unhappiness. Develop a personal relationship with Jesus through a dedicated prayer life. Most certainly, our Lord will bless you with the Holy Spirit's gifts of wisdom, understanding, counsel, fortitude, knowledge, piety, and fear of our Lord. He will further bless you with the fruits of the Holy Spirit: love, joy, peace, patience, kindness, generosity, faithfulness, gentleness, and self-control.

Spiritual Treasures for Reflection

"Now to him who is able to accomplish far more than all we ask or imagine, by the power at work within us." (Eph. 3:20)

"I have strength for everything through him who empowers me." (Phil. 4:13)

The gifts of the Holy Spirit are wisdom, understanding, counsel, fortitude, knowledge, piety, and fear of our Lord. (see Isa. 11:2)

The fruits of the Holy Spirit are love, joy, peace, patience, kindness, generosity, faithfulness, gentleness, and self-control. (see Gal. 5:22–23)

Personal Notes of Reflection

_____

_____

_____

_____

_____

Chapter 16

What Is God Calling Me to Do with My Life?

The Baptism of our oldest son, Blake, was performed by Deacon Ed Dragon. I didn't know much about deacons in the Church before that. But at the Baptism, I had a fleeting thought that God might ask me to serve Him in this role one day. Twenty years later, after our youngest son, Grant, started high school, I was teaching religion to sixth-grade students at St. Ann School when the thought occurred to me to consider the diaconate. Shortly thereafter, I met with our pastor and deacon regarding this possible calling. Both told me to pray to God about whether this was His plan for me. At the time, my law practice was very busy, and we had many family obligations. I wondered if God was truly calling me to the diaconate or if this was just my imagination. Over the next few years, I prayed to God that He would guide me according to His plan for my future. The response from our Lord was to apply for the diaconate, and work and family time would take care of themselves. God has truly blessed me over the last twelve years, both in my formation for the diaconate and in my time serving Him as a deacon at Good Shepherd Parish in New Orleans.

Did you know that God has a specific mission for each of us that He developed before the beginning of the world? St. Paul said, "He chose us in him, before the foundation of the world, to be holy and without blemish before him" (Eph. 1:4). The prophet Jeremiah further describes the plan God has for us: "For I know well the plans I have in mind for you, says the LORD, plans for your welfare, not for woe! plans to give you a future of hope" (Jer. 29:11). It is amazing to know that even before we were born, God set aside roles for us in His earthly kingdom.

In Luke's Gospel, we learn that Jesus answered the call from God to begin His public ministry when He was baptized by His cousin John the Baptist in the Jordan River. The Holy Spirit descended upon Jesus in bodily form like a dove. God the Father spoke from Heaven that day, informing everyone that Jesus was the Messiah when He said, "You are my beloved Son; with you I am well pleased" (Luke 3:22).

Numerous others have accepted God's plan for them. In response to a message from God through the Angel Gabriel, our Blessed Mother Mary agreed to be the Mother of Jesus. Let us recall her words, "Behold, I am the handmaid of the Lord. May it be done to me according to your word" (Luke 1:38). Eleven of the original twelve apostles freely accepted the call from Jesus to give up their lives, leave their homeland, and spread the good news of the Gospel. St. Teresa Benedicta of the Cross became a Carmelite sister at the request of Jesus. One of her wonderful messages was, "Surrender without reservation to the Lord who has called us. This is required of us so that the face of the earth may be renewed."[13]

---

[13] Fr. Pat McCloskey, O.F.M., "Holy Quotes from Catholic Saints," Franciscan Spirit/FranciscanMedia.org.

So what is God's plan for each of us? Are we willing to say yes to the mission that He has for us? Are we willing to put God's will before ours? Perhaps some of us are in a state of uncertainty without a clear path forward, or maybe we are living a life of boredom with no real direction. Only our Lord can help us with the direction we need.

Jesus may be calling you to consider one or more of the following roles to fulfill His plan for you:

- Accept a Sacrament of Service to others through Marriage or through Holy Orders as a priest or deacon, or serve the Church as a religious. The Sacrament of Marriage includes a lifetime commitment to your spouse and the willingness to bring children into the world and raise them in the practice of faith. Holy Orders and service as a religious are agreements to deny oneself and serve the needs of others.
- Work a job to support your family and donate to charitable causes.
- Participate in a church ministry that helps our Lord's neediest souls, such as serving meals in a homeless shelter, serving the Eucharist to patients in hospitals and nursing homes, visiting prisoners in jail, or cooking for families who have lost loved ones.
- Take care of an aging parent or family member on a daily or regular basis.
- Be bold and spread the good news of your faith to encourage family members and friends to come back to the Church.
- Serve as a role model for others by the way you live, imitating Jesus, practicing His virtues, and avoiding the sinful temptations of the world.

- Lead or participate in a weekly or monthly Bible study or spiritual book club with your family members, friends, or church members.
- Pray daily prayers such as the Rosary with your spouse and your children.

Spend some time over the next few weeks and months discerning the calling that Jesus has for you to serve Him. Perhaps seek the advice of a trusted family member, friend, priest, or deacon in considering your plan. Pray to our Lord for His guidance and direction. Please say yes to His call, as He needs each one of us to make a difference for Him in a culture that is truly starved for more of His disciples.

The prophet Isaiah describes God's plan for us this way:

> I, the LORD, have called you for the victory
> of justice,
> I have grasped you by the hand;
> I formed you, and set you
> as a covenant for the people,
> a light for the nations,
> To open the eyes of the blind,
> to bring out prisoners from confinement,
> and from the dungeon, those who live in
> darkness. (Isa. 42:6–7)

To truly answer God's call, we have to abandon our will and accept His will for our lives. Through the Psalms, God tells us, "Teach me to do your will, for you are my God. May your kind spirit guide me on ground that is level" (Ps. 143:10).

St. Teresa of Calcutta visited St. Michael Special School in New Orleans in 1976. This school was founded by the School Sisters of Notre Dame with support from the Archdiocese of New

Orleans and is dedicated to serving children and young adults with intellectual and developmental disabilities. After her visit, St. Teresa wrote a letter to her hosts, thanking them for their hospitality. She ended her letter with these simple words: "Pray much for me, that my yes to Jesus is always with a big smile."[14]

---

[14] Letter kept in a the room occupied by the Saint during her visit to St. Michael Special School in New Orleans.

Spiritual Treasures for Reflection

"For I know well the plans I have in mind for you, says the LORD, plans for your welfare, not for woe! plans to give you a future of hope." (Jer. 29:11)

"Behold, I am the handmaid of the Lord. May it be done to me according to your word." (Luke 1:38)

"Surrender without reservation to the Lord who has called us. This is required of us so that the face of the earth may be renewed." (St. Teresa Benedicta of the Cross)

Personal Notes of Reflection

_____

_____

_____

_____

_____

Chapter 17

Evolving into a Rock for Jesus

My father, Rudy Eason, was from Monroe, Louisiana, and the youngest of four boys. All the Eason brothers, Dick, Frank, Bill, and Rudy, served in World War II. My uncle Dick was a Navy fighter pilot whose plane was shot down during a bombing raid over Japan shortly before the war ended. They were tough men who were part of what has become known as the "Greatest Generation." Later in life, when his only remaining brother, Bill, died, my father was in poor health. He was a leg amputee suffering from severe heart disease and diabetes. At the funeral for Bill, the family was very upset over their loss. During the funeral proceedings, my dad did not shed a tear nor show any emotion. On the long drive home after the services, I asked him how he handled the grief for his brother. He said, "Someone had to be a rock for the family."

During our time on earth, we are on a spiritual journey. It begins with Baptism when Original Sin is wiped away and we are blessed with the gifts and fruits of the Holy Spirit (CCC 1263, 1266). The spiritual journey on earth ends at death, when our souls will be judged by our Lord. Jesus wants us to evolve over time to become a rock for Him so we can spend eternity in Heaven. He wants us to lead other souls to Him by performing the daily mission He has for each of us.

Two of the greatest rocks for Jesus are St. Peter and St. Paul. Over time, both saints evolved into rocks for our Lord. We know about the spiritual lives of these men through the New Testament. The growth and development of St. Peter is described in the Gospels. Similarly, our knowledge of St. Paul comes from the Acts of the Apostles and the many letters that he wrote to the Romans, Corinthians, Ephesians, and others.

Originally a fisherman, St. Peter was one of the first apostles chosen by Jesus. During the three years of our Lord's public ministry, St. Peter had growing pains in his spiritual development. There were several instances when he fell short of being a rock for Jesus. He denied knowing our Lord three times, impulsively cut off the ear of a soldier, and demonstrated little faith while in a boat during a storm on the Sea of Galilee.

Shortly before Jesus was crucified, he said to St. Peter, "You are Peter, and upon this rock I will build my church" (Matt. 16:18). After Jesus was executed, the Holy Spirit was at work in St. Peter's life, and he became the rock that Jesus called him to be. He was the first pope of Rome and led the early Church. Because of St. Peter's faith, Emperor Nero martyred him by crucifying him upside down in the Circus arena for the enjoyment of the crowds.

The story of the spiritual evolution of St. Paul begins with his role as a Roman soldier who presided over the persecutions of many of the early Christians, including the martyrdom of St. Stephen. One day, while St. Paul was on the road to Damascus, a light from the sky flashed around him, and he was blinded for three days. This experience jolted him into becoming a rock for our Lord. He evolved from being a persecutor of Christians to a strong supporter of them. St. Paul became an apostle and preached that our Lord was the Son of God and the Messiah. This saint was instrumental in establishing several churches during his travels. He remained in contact with the faithful in these churches, often writing letters promoting the values of Jesus. Many of his letters are part of the books of the New Testament. In AD 67, St. Paul visited Rome, where he was arrested, and Emperor Nero ordered him decapitated.

In the New Testament, St. Peter describes Jesus' call for our transition. He tells us that we can share in God's divine nature and escape from the corruption of the world. "Make every effort to supplement your faith with virtue, virtue with knowledge, knowledge with self-control, self-control with endurance, endurance with devotion, devotion with mutual affection, mutual affection with love" (2 Pet. 1:5–7). Our Lord wants us to transition to a state of love for Him.

So where are we in the transition process? Are we living in a state of corruption from the world, with weaknesses of anger, fear, greed, misconduct, lack of self-discipline, jealousy, lust, or self-pride? Have we started the conversion toward becoming a "rock" for God by replacing our vices with the virtues of courage, prudence, self-control, justice, fortitude, faith, hope, and love? Have we eliminated the vices and are now living by the virtues?

During the time of our Lord's public ministry, He came upon a blind man who was practicing the virtue of faith. In chapter 10 of Mark's Gospel, Jesus was leaving the town of Jericho with the disciples and a sizable crowd. He came across a man on the side of the road named Bartimaeus. As Jesus was walking, Bartimaeus twice said, "Jesus, son of David, have pity on me" (Mark 10:47). The apostles called out to Bartimaeus, summoning him to Jesus. The blind man went to our Lord, who said to him, "What do you want me to do for you?" (Mark 10:51). Bartimaeus answered, "'Master, I want to see.' Jesus told him, 'Go your way; your faith has saved you'" (Mark 10:51, 52). Immediately, Bartimaeus received his sight and followed Jesus. He was a rock for Jesus by living a faith-filled life.

Our Lord was a rock for His Father, because He spent His whole life practicing virtues, especially during His Passion. From His time in the Garden of Gethsemane, Jesus willingly accepted His execution. He never wavered from His commitment to be a rock for God. Frequently, He even asked God to forgive those who took His life.

In simple terms, being a rock for Jesus means living a virtuous life by always pursuing and promoting spiritual excellence and by doing His will in all that we think, say, and do. It is time to evolve into a life with our Lord in control. We must keep our focus on Jesus and not on earthly ways.

Spiritual Treasures for Reflection

"You are Peter, and upon this rock I will build My Church." (Matt. 16:18)

"Make every effort to supplement your faith with virtue, virtue with knowledge, knowledge with self-control, self-control with endurance, endurance with devotion, devotion with mutual affection, mutual affection with love." (2 Pet. 1:5–7)

"Go your way; your faith has saved you." (Mark 10:52)

Personal Notes of Reflection

_____

_____

_____

_____

_____

Chapter 18

The Intercessory Power of
Our Blessed Mother Mary

In the laundry room of our home, there are several shelves. One of the shelves stores items we use daily, such as car keys, cell phones, and wallets. The other shelves hold items that we use occasionally, such as a flashlight, suntan lotion, and different types of hats.

Many of us tend to forget about our Blessed Mother, putting her on a spiritual shelf and only occasionally recognizing her on her feast days, such as the Immaculate Conception, the Assumption of Mary, and the Mother of God. This is a huge oversight, as we all need Our Lady on a daily basis as part of our spiritual lives to draw closer to Jesus. She is the greatest woman who ever lived and the best intercessor to Jesus.

In this chapter, we will explore the role of our Blessed Mother in the Church, how she can become a big part of our daily spiritual lives, and the importance of asking her to intercede to her Son, Jesus, for our prayer requests.

The role of Our Lady in the Church began with her commitment to be the holy Mother of Jesus. As mentioned before, in response to the angel Gabriel who asked her to be the Mother of Jesus, Mary said, "Behold, I am the handmaid of the Lord. May it be done to me according to your word" (Luke 1:38). Imagine the pressure on Our Lady to serve God in this way. She had to place her trust in God, because she had no idea what her life would be like. She had the responsibility to raise Jesus in the practice of the faith. Perhaps her biggest challenge was to be perfect, living without sin. She experienced the greatest joys in life with the birth of her Son, Jesus, raising Him and observing His public life bringing the good news to others. Conversely, our Blessed Mother experienced the greatest sadness when she observed her Son being tortured and crucified for false accusations.

The Gospels have several passages about Our Lady which help us to fully understand her role in our lives. When Jesus was dying on the Cross, He told the disciples that she would be our spiritual Mother. He said, "Behold, your mother" (John 19:27). Blessed Mother Mary demonstrated for us how to be a true servant of Jesus, doing His will always. She said, "Do whatever he [Jesus] tells you" (John 2:5). Furthermore, Our Lady tells us to spread the good news to others to bring them closer to Jesus. She said, "My soul proclaims the greatness of the Lord; my spirit rejoices in God my savior" (Luke 1:46–47). Also, Our Lady foreshadows her future apparitions around the world when she says, "Behold, from now on will all ages call me blessed" (Luke 1:48).

The Mother of Jesus was perfect in her earthly life, as she did not sin (CCC 411). After her death, she was assumed into Heaven body and soul to be with her Son for eternity (CCC 966, 969). There she was crowned Queen of Heaven by Jesus to help all souls get to Heaven (Rev. 12:1–5; CCC 968, 969, 975). To fulfill her heavenly responsibilities, down through the centuries, Our Lady has made appearances all over the world.

One of her apparitions is known as *Our Lady of the Miraculous Medal*. On July 18, 1830, Blessed Mother Mary appeared to

St. Catherine Laboure in the chapel in the motherhouse of the Daughters of Charity in France. They talked for over two hours. One of the messages to St. Catherine was to create a medal, as soon as possible, with the Blessed Mother's image on it. Our Lady promised that all who wear the medal would receive great graces. The expression on the medal states: "O Mary conceived without sin, pray for us who have recourse to thee."

Another apparition is known as *Our Lady of Fátima*. On October 13, 1917, Our Lady appeared to Lúcia dos Santos and her two cousins Francisco and Jacinta Marto, in Fátima, Portugal, on six occasions. These three children are now saints in the Church. One of Our Lady's messages was to pray the Rosary each day to obtain peace for the world.

On February 11, 1850, Our Blessed Mother Mary appeared to St. Bernadette Soubirous in a tiny grotto known as Massabielle near Lourdes, France. At the time of this first apparition, known as *Our Lady of Lourdes*, St. Bernadette fell to her knees and prayed the Rosary. Our Lady appeared to St. Bernadette on several occasions. One of her messages was to do penance and pray for sinners. Thousands of pilgrims visit the Grotto each year. Over seventy miracles have been attributed to the Blessed Mother by pilgrims visiting the shrine.

Our Blessed Mother Mary is the role model for St. Teresa of Calcutta and all the sisters in her religious order, the Missionaries of Charity. The sisters pray to Our Lady fervently as a symbol of great holiness, purity, chastity, surrender, and sacred motherhood. Here is the prayer created by St. Teresa to the Blessed Mother:

Mary, Mother of Jesus, give me your heart, so beautiful, so pure, so immaculate, so full of love and humility that

I may receive Jesus in the bread of life, love Him as you loved Him and serve Him in the distressing disguise of the poorest of the poor.[15]

So how can we remove our Blessed Mother Mary from our spiritual shelf to become a major part of our daily lives? There are numerous prayers that we can say, which include the Rosary, Hail Holy Queen, the Memorare, the Chaplet of Our Lady of Mercy, and the Angelus. Additionally, we can consecrate our souls to Our Lady. In the early 1700s, St. Louis de Montfort wrote the *Treatise on True Devotion to the Blessed Virgin*. It was first published in 1843 and is considered one of the greatest books ever written about Our Blessed Mother Mary. The premise of the treatise is that the shortest path to Jesus is through devotion to His Mother Mary. It consists of prayers and readings over a thirty-three-day period to totally consecrate our souls to Our Lady. Over the years, eight popes have consecrated themselves to her.

St. Louis de Montfort wrote in his treatise about his relationship to the Blessed Mother:

I am all yours, and all that I have is yours, O loving Jesus, through Mary, Your most holy Mother.... But my labor will be rewarded if this little book falls into the hands of a noble soul, a child of God and of Mary, born not out of blood nor the will of the flesh nor of the will of man. My time will be well spent if, by the grace of the Holy Spirit, after having read this book he is convinced of the supreme value of the solid devotion to Mary.[16]

---

[15] Lucinda Vardey, *A Simple Path by Mother Teresa* (New York: Ballantine Books, 1995), XXV.

[16] *Treatise on True Devotion to the Blessed Virgin*, nos. 216, 112.

Pope St. John Paul II wrote about his devotion to Our Lady. He states, "The motto *Totus tuus* is inspired by the teaching of St. Louis Marie Grignion de Montfort. These two words express total belonging to Jesus through Mary."[17] Consecrating our souls to our Blessed Mother Mary is a spiritual game changer.

Our Lady is always there for us to intercede to her Son, Jesus, for specific prayer requests for family and friends (CCC 2677, 2679). The mother of Jesus is a source of grace for all who pray to her (CCC 966, 968).

My mother-in-law, Mary Ann Doyle, is eighty-eight years old and lives in an assisted living center in Washington, Indiana. She experiences major pain daily after undergoing many medical procedures, including two knee replacements, lower back surgery, and hip replacement. She also suffers from heart disease. When the pain gets severe, she prays to Our Lady, who gives her the grace of peace that she needs to manage her pain.

Over the centuries, numerous souls have received all kinds of graces from our Blessed Mother Mary. In 1605, St. Vincent de Paul was sailing as a passenger on a ship when it was taken captive by Barbary pirates who sold him into slavery. Subsequently, he was resold as a slave several times to different owners over a period of two years. During this time, he prayed to Our Lady for her intercession. He was able to escape in 1607.

Blessed Francis Xavier Seelos began taking courses at the University of Munich in 1841. During that year, Our Lady appeared to him and told him to become a missionary. Following this direction, he applied to the Redemptorist order in the United States to become a missionary. In 1843, he went to the

---

[17] John Paul II, letter to the Montfort religious family (December 8, 2003), no. 1.

Redemptorist seminary in Baltimore, Maryland and remained in the United States for the rest of his life. Yellow fever broke out in New Orleans in the fall of 1867, causing 5,000 deaths. After visiting a man dying from the disease, Francis was overcome by it and died on October 4, 1867.

The ending of our prayer to the Blessed Mother is "pray for us sinners, now and at the hour of our death." The Mother of Jesus will be there for us while we are in this life and at the hour of our death. She was always there for Jesus when He was in this life and was with Him at the hour of His death. Our Lady will be there for us in the same way if we pray to her.

To think of our Blessed Mother Mary only occasionally on her feast days is a huge oversight. Please consider a daily place for her in your spiritual life. Remember, there are many prayers to say to her, such as the Rosary, the Hail Holy Queen, the Memorare, the Chaplet of Our Lady of Mercy, and the Angelus. We can consecrate our souls to her as well. Most importantly, we can ask for her intercession for family and friends who may be suffering in this life.

Spiritual Treasures for Reflection

"Do whatever He [Jesus] tells you." (John 2:5)

"Mary said, 'Behold, I am the handmaid of the Lord. May it be done to me according to your word.'" (Luke 1:38)

"My soul proclaims the greatness of the Lord; my spirit rejoices in God my savior." (Luke 1:46–47)

Personal Notes of Reflection

_____

_____

_____

_____

_____

Chapter 19

Restoring Our Families to Holiness — JMJ

Bill and Kathy Johnson have two teenage children, Christy and Jack. Both parents work full time and don't get home until dinner. The Johnsons live in a nice area of town. Bill and Kathy are working to save money to buy a boat that they have always wanted. Christy and Jack are doing average work in high school. After school, Christy visits with her friends, sometimes drinking alcohol and listening to music, and Jack likes to play video games with the boys in his neighborhood. In the evening, the family usually entertains themselves with television or social media. The teenagers don't like to do very much homework. None of the Johnson family members spend time in daily prayer. They don't attend Sunday Mass outside of Christmas and Easter, as they don't seem to have time for it. On the weekends, they often go their separate ways, doing many activities individually.

One Saturday night, Christy was driving home from a school dance and was stopped by the police. The investigating officer found alcohol in Christy's car and discovered that she had been drinking. She was arrested and charged with a DUI. A few weeks later, Jack was suspended from school for bullying another student. These events served as a wakeup call to Bill and Kathy that their family was in trouble. The Johnson family had lost their way, and Bill and Kathy began searching for the path to become a better family.

It seems that in America today, many families have strayed from a path of holiness to become dysfunctional. Why is this? Our society seems intent on destroying the family unit by the plagues of divorce, relativism, and secularization. The desire for material wealth often consumes parents. This results in parents ignoring the responsibility of properly raising their children. Many families are run by a single parent with the other parent having abandoned their duties. Some children are raised without discipline, and their futures are dashed by abuse or neglect. Too often, families don't take the time to have dinner together, pray at the end of the day, or attend Mass on Sunday. Social media frequently interferes with quality interaction between parents and their children. The focus becomes the enjoyment of the individual and not the family unit.

To counteract the negative influences of our culture on families, we need to examine the Christian values that will help families find their way back to holiness. The first place to start is to focus on the family as a unit and not as an afterthought. The family must come first in everything. Building a relationship of love and sharing begins with each family member's desire to offer himself for the sake of the others. Our lives must be centered on service to our family members. The parents set the tone of joy and happiness each day by their total commitment to the family. The children do their part by taking direction from their parents and contribute to the family unit as they can. St. Paul tells us that whoever does not provide for family members "has denied the faith and is worse than an unbeliever" (1 Tim. 5:8).

The most important element of a holy family is the commitment to the practice of the faith. The prophet Joshua described the issue this way: "As for me and my household, we will serve the Lord" (Josh. 24:15). This commitment begins with daily prayer. It is imperative that the family pray together before meals and at bedtime each day. There are many books that contain Bible stories for children. Reading a story to the children before bedtime is very helpful for educating them in the Faith. Encourage children to pray for others who may need the help of our Lord. When our son Grant was a young boy, his prayer list was so broad that it even included his pet turtles Spike, Speedy, and Zephyr. As children become teenagers, set aside time for them on Sunday nights for Bible study or praying the Rosary, or both. For some, this recitation can become a lifelong habit, as it has been for a deacon friend whose family continued the tradition even after his kids were married and living separately.

Attendance at Mass on Sundays is a must for families. Even when we are on vacation, we must go to Mass. This obligation not only keeps us firm in our faith but also emphasizes the importance of Jesus to our families. Likewise, it is vital that members of the family participate in the Mass. Children can serve as altar servers, and parents can participate as lectors or Eucharistic ministers.

Fr. Joe Kraft, a professor of pastoral theology at Notre Dame Seminary, created the Faith Society. The word *faith* is an acronym for "Family Altar in the Home." Fr. Kraft suggests that setting up a special place for an altar in the home helps the family gather for prayer and time dedicated to God. The altar can be very simple. He suggests that it can include a small table that has linens, a crucifix, holy water, a Rosary, candles, holy cards, the Bible, statues, prayer books, and pictures of family members and friends to pray for.

The success of the family unit begins with the husband and wife. They must agree to commit to the practice of their faith and then pursue it together. There must be mutual respect for the role of one another in these efforts. St. Paul tells us, "Husbands, love your wives, even as Christ loved the church" (Eph. 5:25). He further says that husbands are to avoid any bitterness toward their wives (Col. 3:19).

Parents, whether married or single, have defined responsibilities to their children. The duty of parents to help their children is primordial and inalienable (CCC 2221). Parents must regard them as "*children of God* and respect them as *human persons*" (CCC 2222). They are required to educate their children to fulfill God's law (CCC 2222). Parents are to create a home where "tenderness, forgiveness, respect, fidelity, and disinterested service are the rule. The home is well suited for *education in the virtues*" (CCC 2223).

Similarly, parents are to serve as great role models for their children. It is well known that children often imitate their parents. Parents are to educate their children in the Faith and provide for their physical and spiritual needs (CCC 2226, 2228). It is important that parents encourage their kids to participate in a variety of activities to broaden their knowledge of the world and to develop social skills. Children can be easily influenced in a negative way by others, thereby requiring parents to monitor the individuals that they befriend. Parents must be willing to drop everything to protect their children from situations that may harm them. Parents have to be true shepherds of their children.

Rosalyn and I raised three boys. We learned that one way to help them focus on Christian values was to post a set of Eason family rules on our refrigerator door. We knew that these boys would see these rules often, as they were always searching the refrigerator for something to eat. The rules are as follows: no grumps allowed, always do your best, always do what is right, and no trash-talking ever. Even though our boys are now men and living on their own, these rules remain posted on our refrigerator door as a reminder for us and for them.

One of the Ten Commandments is to honor your father and mother (Exod. 20:12). Respect for parents "fills the home with light and warmth" (CCC 2219). On the other hand, children have the duty to observe the commands of their father and accept the teaching of their mothers (Prov. 6:20). They are to be obedient to their parents. Jesus was the great role model for obedience to His foster father, Joseph, and His Mother, Mary (Luke 2:51). Obedience develops the virtue of humility and is at the core of holiness. Children are not perfect, but we must hold them accountable for their actions.

Jesus, His Blessed Mother, Mary, and St. Joseph are recognized as the Holy Family in our Catholic Faith. At its core, this family practiced Christian values that are described in the New Testament. These Christian values are the difference between a family being holy or dysfunctional. The Holy Family is so important that our Church celebrates a feast day for them every year between Christmas and New Year's Day. Also, a common practice is to write the letters "JMJ"—Jesus, Mary, Joseph—at the top of correspondence and memos in remembrance of the Holy Family.

The movement in our culture toward the loss of the family unit must be stopped. The dysfunctional family is often filled with unnecessary hatred, stress, worry, and jealousy. Restoring our families to a state of holiness by practicing Christian values will bring back the great joy, happiness, and peace that our Lord intended for us. JMJ.

Spiritual Treasures for Reflection

"As for me and my household, we will serve the Lord."
(Josh. 24:15)

"And whoever does not provide for relatives and especially family members has denied the faith and is worse than an unbeliever." (1 Tim. 5:8)

Parents are to create a home where "tenderness, forgiveness, respect, fidelity and disinterested service are the rule. The home is well suited for education in the virtues." (CCC 2223)

Personal Notes of Reflection

_____

_____

_____

_____

_____

Chapter 20

There Is Forgiveness for
Our Sins and Mercy from God

In a television commercial for a car insurance company, a teenager is involved in a minor vehicle accident for the first time. He speaks with his parents about the incident, trying to downplay it to minimize any potential punishment. The teenager portrays a very humble appearance in the presence of his parents. His mother has many choices as to how to respond to the circumstances. She can be angry, scream at him, and tell him to pay for the damages. Or she can show him compassion and mercy. The mother chooses compassion and mercy and suspends his driving privileges for a month. The son leaves the room with a sigh of relief that his mother had mercy.

At times, we have all been in a position to seek mercy from others for our harmful ways. Students in school seek forgiveness for their misconduct in the classroom. Spouses seek mercy from each other for spending money that exceeds the family budget, for coming home late from an event, for failing to do a chore timely, or for canceling a vacation because of a work situation. Workers sometimes seek forgiveness from their supervisors for missing a deadline. None of us is perfect, and at times we need forgiveness from others.

Spiritual Excellence

In our spiritual lives, we need forgiveness and mercy from our Lord for sins that we commit against Him. In St. Paul's letters in the New Testament, he lists sins that offend our Lord. In Romans, the sins listed are wickedness, evil, greed, malice, envy, murder, rivalry, treachery, spite, gossips, and scandalmongers (Rom. 1:29–30). In Galatians, there are other sins such as immorality, impurity, idolatry, sorcery, hatred, jealousy, anger, selfishness, dissensions, factions, drinking bouts, and orgies (Gal. 5:19–21).

The Ten Commandments describe the sins of idolatry, misusing the Lord's name, murder, adultery, theft, bearing false witness against others, and coveting neighbors' property (Exod. 20:1–17). Because of the free will God gave us, living sin-free is quite a challenge. We truly need forgiveness and mercy from God for our misconduct. Is there real forgiveness for our sins and mercy for our souls from God? The answer is most assuredly yes. Jesus came into the world to teach us His way of life in order to help us avoid sinful conduct. He was crucified, died, and was buried for the forgiveness of our sins. By His death, He gave all those who eagerly await Him an opportunity for salvation (Heb. 9:26–28; CCC 456, 457, 519).

In Luke's Gospel, our Lord teaches us about His mercy for transgressions by forgiving a woman for her sins. While Jesus was in the house of a Pharisee for dinner, the woman began to wash His feet with her tears. Then she wiped His feet, kissed them, and anointed them. Jesus said these words to those at the table: "So I tell you, her many sins have been forgiven; hence, she has shown great love" (Luke 7:47).

Forgiveness and mercy for our sins is one of our Lord's most important spiritual messages. He demonstrated this through His direct communication with St. Maria Faustina Kowalska. This saint was the third of ten children born into a poor family in Poland. She became a religious in the Congregation of the Sisters of Our Lady of Mercy and is considered one of the outstanding Mystics of the Church.

For much of her life, St. Maria kept a diary in which she recorded her communications with Jesus. In her diary, she described her mission to proclaim Christ's mercy. Our Lord said to her,

> I am sending you with My mercy to the people of the whole world. I do not want to punish aching mankind, but I desire to heal it, pressing it to My Merciful Heart.... You are the secretary of My mercy. I have chosen you for that office in this life and the next life.... To make known to souls the great mercy I have for them and to exhort them to trust in the bottomless depth of My mercy.[18]

St. Maria gave us the image of the merciful Jesus as well. In her diary, she recorded a vision she had of Jesus. She wrote:

> I saw the Lord Jesus clothed in a white garment. One hand raised in the gesture of blessing, the other was touching the garment at the breast. From beneath the garment, slightly drawn aside from at the breast, there were emanating two large rays, one red, the other pale.... After a while, Jesus said to me, "Paint an image according to the pattern you see, with the signature: Jesus, I trust in You.... I want this image ... to be solemnly blessed on the first Sunday after Easter; that Sunday is to be the Feast of Mercy."[19]

---

[18] *Diary of Saint Maria Faustina Kowalska* (Stockbridge, MA: Marian Press, 2012), nos. 1588, 1605, 1567.

[19] *Diary*, nos. 47, 49.

The image described by St. Maria with the words "Jesus, I trust in You" was painted by an artist and now appears in thousands of churches around the world.

On April 3, 2000, Pope St. John Paul II canonized Bl. Maria Faustina Kowalska as a saint. During his homily that day, he declared that the second Sunday of Easter will be known as Divine Mercy Sunday. The Catholic Church now celebrates this day throughout the world.

The spiritual concept of mercy has been described by Pope Francis. He declared a Jubilee Year of Mercy from December 8, 2015, to November 20, 2016. At the conclusion of the Year of Mercy, Pope Francis wrote an apostolic letter entitled *Misericordia et Misera*. In this letter, the Holy Father says:

> *Forgiveness* is the most visible sign of the Father's love, which Jesus sought to reveal by His entire life. Every page of the Gospel is marked by this imperative of a love that loves to the point of forgiveness. Even at the last moment of His earthly life, as He was being nailed to the cross, Jesus spoke words of forgiveness, "Father, forgive them; for they know not what they do" (Luke 23:34). Nothing of what a repentant sinner places before God's mercy can be excluded from the embrace of His forgiveness. For this reason, none of us has the right to make forgiveness conditional. Mercy is always a gratuitous act of our heavenly Father, an unconditional and unmerited act of love. Consequently, we cannot risk opposing the full freedom of the love which God enters into the life of every person.[20]

---

[20] Pope Francis, Apostolic Letter *Misericordia et Misera* (November 2016), no. 2.

One of the seven sacraments of the Church is Reconciliation, or Confession. This sacrament gives us the opportunity to seek forgiveness for our sins from our Lord and the purification of our souls. The *Catechism of the Catholic Church* describes Jesus as the physician of our soul (CCC 1421). Furthermore, "those who approach the sacrament of Penance obtain pardon from God's mercy for the offense committed against Him" (CCC 1422). Through the Sacrament of Penance, we are reconciled with God (CCC 980). It restores us to God's grace and joins us with Him in an intimate friendship (CCC 1468).

This important sacrament is often forgotten or overlooked by many. Some consider it a challenge to contemplate all the aspects of our sinfulness and then confess these sins to a priest. Confession is an acknowledgment of our weaknesses. But it is crystal clear that the rewards of peace and grace from our Lord following Confession far outweigh any perceived challenge.

Participating in the Sacrament of Penance on a regular basis, for instance monthly, will result in a true conversion of our souls. A monthly examination of our souls often reveals repetition of the same sins against Jesus. It is truly embarrassing to confess the same transgressions over and over again because we don't have the self-discipline to overcome them. Over time, by the grace of Jesus, we can cure these repetitious sins, thereby truly purifying our souls and bringing unparalleled joy and peace to our hearts. At the end of the Sacrament of Reconciliation, or Confession, we seek forgiveness for our sins by saying the Act of Contrition:

> O my God, I am heartily sorry for having offended Thee, and I detest all my sins because of Thy just punishments, but most of all because they offend Thee, my God, who art all good and deserving of all my love. I firmly resolve

with the help of Thy grace to sin no more and to avoid the near occasion of sin. Amen.

An additional suggestion for Confession is to kneel before a life-size crucifix in church while praying our penance. Gazing at our suffering Jesus, knowing that He was tortured to death for our sins, gives us the resolve to sin no more. It is painful to realize that our sins hurt our Lord and Savior so much. A sincere confession and praying the Act of Contrition instill great peace in our hearts, as we know that our sins have been forgiven by the mercy of God. Forgiveness of our sins and mercy from God are real. Our Lord, as well as His saints and our pope, have confirmed this. All we have to do is to make a sincere confession.

Spiritual Treasures for Reflection

"So I tell you, her many sins have been forgiven; hence, she has shown great love." (Luke 7:47)

"I am sending you with My mercy to the people of the whole world. I do not want to punish aching mankind, but I desire to heal it, pressing it to My Merciful Heart." (St. Maria Faustina Kowalska)

"To make known to souls the great Mercy I have for them and to exhort them to trust in the bottomless depth of My mercy." (St. Maria Faustina Kowalska)

Through the Sacrament of Confession, we are reconciled with God. It restores us to God's grace and joins us with Him in an intimate friendship. (see CCC 980, 1468)

Personal Notes of Reflection

_____

_____

_____

_____

_____

Chapter 21

The Holy Eucharist Is
Nourishment for Our Souls

The people of New Orleans give considerable time and attention
to the subject of food. They talk about internationally known
chefs like Emeril Lagasse, Susan Spicer, and Andrea Apuzzo, to
name a few. There are many famous restaurants in the city, such
as Commander's Palace, Antoine's, Emeril's, and Galatoire's.
Also, there are wonderful neighborhood eating establishments
such as Dooky Chase's, Ye Olde College Inn, and Mother's
Restaurant.

Residents of the city spend countless hours planning meals,
cooking dinners, and eating with family and friends. Cooking
is a hobby for many people who live there. They go to classes,
buy special cooking equipment, and experiment with recipes.
One issue that often arises in discussing the food culture in New
Orleans is the wines. There are often great debates about the
best wines to serve with dinner. By my nonscientific estimation,
the citizens of the city spend one to two hours a day or more on
food matters.

Our bodies require earthly food to function every day. However, we often forget that our souls need nourishment as well.

Jesus tells us that the Holy Eucharist is the nourishment that we need for our souls. In the Gospel of John, Jesus preaches to the crowds about the importance of the Eucharist:

> I am the living bread that came down from heaven; whoever eats this bread will live forever; and the bread that I will give is my flesh for the life of the world.... Amen, amen, I say to you, unless you eat the flesh of the Son of Man and drink his blood, you do not have life within you. Whoever eats my flesh and drinks my blood has eternal life, and I will raise him on the last day. For my flesh is true food, and my blood is true drink. Whoever eats my flesh and drinks my blood remains in me and I in him.... This is the bread that came down from heaven. Unlike your ancestors who ate and still died, whoever eats this bread will live forever. (John 6:51, 53–56, 58)

The Holy Eucharist has been recognized by the Church as having great value for feeding our souls. The Second Vatican Council, in the Dogmatic Constitution of the Church known as *Lumen Gentium*, describes the Eucharist as the source and summit of Christian life.[21]

Pope St. John Paul II declared a Church liturgical celebration known as the Year of the Eucharist from October 2004 through September 2005. Former New Orleans Archbishop Alfred Hughes wrote a letter regarding the Year of the Eucharist in which he said, "On this side of heaven, one cannot experience a more substantial or intense communication with Christ's presence than in the Eucharist." The Eucharist has also been described as

---

[21] Pope Paul VI, Dogmatic Constitution of the Church *Lumen Gentium* (November 1964), no. 11; CCC 1324.

the "magnetic pole" of our existence by Fr. Roger Landry of St. Francis Xavier Church in Hyannis, Massachusetts.

Good Shepherd Parish in New Orleans has twenty parishioners who bring the Holy Eucharist to the patients at two nursing homes, those convalescing at a long-term care hospital, and to those who are homebound. These residents are unable to come to Mass and greatly value receiving our Lord. The comfort and joy they receive from the Blessed Sacrament is overwhelming.

You may remember the story of Miss Ethel from chapter 12. She was a patient at one of the nursing homes in my parish. She could hardly talk and move her body because of the great pain she was experiencing. When we brought the Eucharist to her, she desperately tried to lift her hands to receive it but could not. Upon receiving the Eucharist, there was instant joy on her face. Based on her reaction, there is no doubt that Miss Ethel was receiving the Body of Christ. We are so very thankful to the Eucharistic ministers who serve in our parish and all around the world, as they are truly making a difference for the souls who can't come to Mass, as they provide them spiritual nourishment.

Caffeine energy drinks have been promoted as giving people a physical lift during the day. Coffee products are used for this purpose as well. Why not receive the Eucharist during the week for a spiritual boost for our souls? After all, the Mass and the Eucharist are offered every day of the year.

The Holy Eucharist has been the subject of many spiritual events over the years. St. Margaret Mary Alacoque, a French religious who lived in the 1600s, received private revelations from Jesus. Our Lord told her that He had many promises for the souls in a state of grace that receive the Eucharist on the first Friday of

nine consecutive months. This has become known as the First
Friday Devotion. Our Lord made these promises:

- I will give them all the graces necessary in their state
  of life.
- I will establish peace in their homes.
- I will comfort them in all their afflictions.
- I will be their secure refuge during life and, above all,
  in death.
- I will bestow a large blessing upon all of their undertakings.
- Sinners will find in My Heart the source and the infinite
  ocean of mercy.
- Tepid souls shall grow fervent.
- Fervent souls shall quickly mount to high perfection.
- I will bless every place where a picture of My Heart shall
  be set up and honored.
- I will give to priests the gifts of touching the most hard-
  ened hearts.
- Those who shall promote this devotion shall have their
  names written in My Heart, never to be effaced.
- I promise you in the excessive mercy of My Heart that
  My all-powerful love will grant to all those who communicate on the First Friday in nine consecutive months the
  grace of final penitence; they shall not die in My disgrace
  nor without receiving their sacraments; My Divine Heart
  shall be their safe refuge in this last moment.[22]

There was a priest who lived in Lanciano, Italy, in the eighth
century who had doubts about whether Jesus was truly present
in the Eucharist. During Mass one day, when he was saying the

---

[22] Fr. Edward McNamara, "First Friday Devotion and First Friday,"
EWTN, March 17, 2015.

Prayer of Consecration, he saw the bread and wine converted into human Flesh and Blood. This has come to be known as the Eucharistic Miracle of Lanciano. This supernatural event was the subject of an investigation by the local archbishop. It was later approved as a miracle by the Church. The Flesh and Blood are still preserved in an exhibit in the Church of San Francisco in Lanciano, Italy. In 1971, a professor of anatomy, Odoardo Linoli, performed an analysis of the Flesh. The test results revealed that it was human cardiac tissue.

St. Maria Faustina Kowalska's full religious name was St. Maria Faustina Kowalska of the Blessed Sacrament. She had numerous apparitions with Jesus and Our Blessed Mother Mary which she wrote about in a diary she kept over the years. One of her entries describes the impact of the Eucharist on her daily life:

> Every morning during meditation, I prepare myself for the whole day's struggle. Holy Communion assures me that I will win the victory.... This bread of the Strong gives me all the strength I need to carry on my mission and the courage to do whatever the Lord asks of me.[23]

Many people have told me over the years that when they receive the Body and Blood of Jesus, they experience a spiritual lift in their souls. I believe this is true. This spiritual joy is on display after Mass every weekend. At Good Shepard Parish in New Orleans, Msgr. Christopher Nalty, Fr. Doug Brougher, and I stand in the back of church after the Mass has ended. We see the smiling faces of the parishioners as they leave church, which demonstrates the power of the Holy Eucharist at work in them. We don't have to wait until the weekend to experience the great

---

[23] *Diary*, no. 91.

spiritual joy of receiving the Holy Eucharist. Mass is offered every day, and so we can participate in this great sacrament daily.

St. Mother Teresa of Calcutta founded the order known as the Missionaries of Charity in 1950. She is known worldwide for her dedication to serving the poorest of the poor. In 1973, her congregation decided to dedicate one hour each day to adoration of the Holy Eucharist. The Eucharist was most important to her. She wrote these words:

> Where will you get the great joy of loving? In the Eucharist, Holy Communion, Jesus has made Himself the Bread of Life to give us life. Night and day, He is there. If you really want to grow in love, come back to the Eucharist, come back to that adoration.[24]

If you are unable to attend Mass during the week because of your schedule, find some time to spend in adoration of the Holy Eucharist at church. Just visiting with Jesus for fifteen minutes will provide great peace and guidance.

Think about it this way. Of all the things we are able to do in life, what activities do we receive the greatest joy and benefit from? These activities can include a vacation, purchasing a new car, going to a concert, or attending a sporting event. But the joy from these trips and events is only temporary. As our memories fade, the joy passes away. Truly, reception of the Body and Blood of our Lord is the best way to attain the greatest joy and happiness. The benefits from the sacrament are not temporary. They last for an eternity. I think back to the photographs of our

[24] Jean Maalouf, *Mother Teresa: Essential Writings* (Ossining, NY: Orbis Books, 2001).

three sons on the days of their First Communion. These pictures are exceptional because you can see the great joy on their faces from receiving the Eucharist for the first time. Their faces could light up a room.

In a book titled *Confessions of a Mega Church Pastor*, a former Methodist minister describes his conversion to the Catholic Faith. Allen Hunt was a pastor of a fifteen-thousand-member church in Alpharetta, Georgia. Pastor Hunt converted to Catholicism because of the church's belief that during the consecration, the bread and wine truly become the Body and Blood of our Lord through the power of the Holy Spirit. Perhaps some of us may not fully believe this truth. Don't cheat yourself out of this true nourishment of body and soul because of some false premise, shaky notion, or misguided comments from peers or friends! Remember, nourishing our souls is just as important as nourishing our bodies. There is no doubt that the Holy Eucharist is spiritual food for our souls.

Spiritual Treasures for Reflection

"Whoever eats my flesh and drinks of my blood has eternal life, and I will raise him on the last day. For my flesh is true food, and my blood is true drink. Whoever eats my flesh and drinks my blood remains in me and I in him." (John 6:54–56)

"Every morning during meditation, I prepare myself for the day's struggle. Holy Communion assures me that I will win the victory.... This bread of the Strong gives me all the strength I need to carry on my mission and the courage to do whatever the Lord asks of me." (St. Maria Faustina Kowalska)

"Where will you get the great joy of loving? In the Eucharist, Holy Communion, Jesus has made Himself the Bread of Life to give us life. Night and day, He is there. If you really want to grow in love, come back to the Eucharist, come back to that adoration." (St. Mother Teresa of Calcutta)

Personal Notes of Reflection

_____

_____

_____

_____

_____

Chapter 22

Finding True and Lasting Divine Peace 24/7

Our country has numerous museums that are dedicated to a wide variety of subjects, including art, history, science, industry, space, and war. New Orleans is home to the well-known National WWII Museum, which memorializes all those who gave their lives defending our country during the Second World War. It has numerous exhibits dedicated to the various theaters of the war that occurred around the world. One of the exhibits features the Paris Peace Treaties signed in 1947. These treaties detailed the peace terms for many countries in Europe at the end of the war. The Paris Peace Treaties brought an end to the terror and fighting for all the nations entering into the accord. Peace was welcomed by these peoples.

Our Lord is calling us to peace as well. His peace is different. It is divine peace that is true and lasting 24/7. Jesus gave the apostles divine peace after He was crucified. In John's Gospel, we learn that three days after Jesus had died, the apostles were locked in the upper room in a state of total fear. They were likely afraid of what would happen to them since Jesus had been crucified. The apostles were concerned for their own safety. Possibly, they regretted leaving their simple lives as carpenters and fishermen.

Our Lord knew their fears. So He appeared and told them not once but twice, "Peace be with you" (John 20:19; 20:21). Jesus showed the apostles His hands and His side to prove to them that He had risen from the dead three days after His Crucifixion, just as He told them.

On February 21, 1931, almost nineteen hundred years after our Lord appeared to the apostles in the upper room, He appeared to St. Maria Faustina Kowalska in a vision in Poland. Recall that in the apparition, Jesus asked St. Faustina to have His image portrayed in a painting with the words "Jesus, I trust in You" inscribed on it. The image that is depicted in the painting is of the risen Lord with His hands and feet bearing the marks of His Crucifixion. St. Faustina wrote Jesus' words in her diary, "The more a soul trusts [in Me], the more [grace] it will receive. Souls that trust boundlessly are a great comfort to Me, because I pour all the treasures of My graces into them."[25]

In order to achieve our Lord's divine peace, we must follow the instruction that Jesus gave to St. Faustina, which is to have 100 percent trust in Him at all times. Learning trust can be difficult due to our life experiences with others. Oftentimes, the people we trust to do certain things or to take care of us fail to do what they are supposed to do. However, the message that Jesus is telling us, through His appearance to St. Faustina, is one of divine trust in Him. This trust is flawless. He is there for us at all times.

Also, divine peace requires us to do God's will and not our own. In 1954, Fr. Anthony Paone wrote the book *My Daily Bread*. The book contains an excellent discussion of spiritual doctrines. It has become so popular that over a million copies have been

[25] *Diary*, no. 1578.

sold. In Fr. Paone's book, he discusses a closer friendship with God. Fr. Paone talks about God when he writes,

> Do not let this earthly life take all of your attention. Think often of Me and of My Will in your life. Then you will become more conscious of My presence within your soul. I bring you the gifts of peace and joy in the Holy Ghost. These gifts are not given to those who pay too much attention to this earthly life…. If I take this step and concentrate more on God's place in my daily life, I shall find the peace of Christ.[26]

By following these two requirements of trusting in Jesus and doing His will, we can have divine peace 24/7. This divine peace is a natural part of our souls.

Frequently, we interrupt our natural divine peace with life issues. We worry about family members, our jobs, or health matters. Sinful behaviors can get the best of us through the abuse of alcohol, drugs, food, money, the mistreatment of others, or lust for another person. Other issues can rob us of our natural divine peace if we allow them to. Earthly desires can divide families. Sometimes, there are inheritance issues, sibling rivalry, or disputes among in-laws. Greed, egos, and pride can consume us. Envy can develop among neighbors simply because one of them has a nicer car or lives in a bigger home.

When did greed, jealousy, egotism, envy, worry, materialism, or sinfulness ever solve an issue or be of help to us? *Never!* In very simple terms, Jesus is telling us that if we continue to live without trusting in Him and doing His will, we lose His divine

---

[26] Fr. Anthony Paone, *My Daily Bread* (Charlotte, NC: TAN Books, 2015), 68, 69.

peace. This causes our Lord great sadness, as His Crucifixion, many miracles, appearance in the upper room to the apostles, and vision to St. Faustina are wasted on us. You see, Jesus desperately wants us to experience His divine peace and joy.

Make no mistake. Divine peace is real! A few years ago, I was in a month-long jury trial defending a company against a defective product claim for $99 million in damages. If we lost the case, a factory was going to close, and four hundred jobs would be lost in a small town. The only way for me to defend the company in the pursuit of justice was to turn total control of our efforts over to our Lord and Savior Jesus Christ. There was no way to defend the claim without having total trust in Jesus and always following His will. I kept a picture of our Lord on a work desk in my hotel room. I prayed daily for guidance and grace from Jesus to obtain justice for our client. As a result of the graces of divine peace and guidance from Jesus, justice was accomplished, and the jobs were saved.

Once you have truly experienced divine peace, you will never go back to earthly ways. Trusting in Jesus and pursuing His will becomes a way of life that is awesome. We can all have true and lasting divine peace 24/7.

Spiritual Treasures for Reflection

"On the evening of that first day of the week, when the doors were locked, where the disciples were, for fear of the Jews, Jesus came and stood in their midst and said to them, 'Peace be with you.'" (John 20:19)

"The more a soul trusts [in Me], the more [grace] it will receive. Souls that trust boundlessly are a great comfort to Me, because I pour all the treasures of My graces into them." (St. Maria Faustina Kowalska)

"Do not let this earthly life take all of your attention. Think often of Me and of My Will in your life. Then you will become more conscious of My presence within your soul. I bring you the gifts of peace and joy in the Holy Ghost. These gifts are not given to those who pay too much attention to this earthly life.... If I take this step and concentrate more on God's place in my life, I shall find the peace of Christ." (Fr. Anthony Paone)

Personal Notes of Reflection

_____

_____

_____

_____

_____

Chapter 23

Experience an Awesome Prayer Life

There are all kinds of exercises for the body. We can walk, jog, swim, bike, lift weights, join exercise classes, and play sports, to name a few. Some exercise for minutes, while others for hours. The goal of all these efforts is to keep our bodies healthy, enjoy an active lifestyle, and live a long life. But what should we do to exercise our souls to keep them healthy and to enjoy a life of peace, joy, and happiness? An awesome prayer life is the answer.

Over the last few years, I have received mixed responses when talking with people about their prayer lives. Some of them say that their prayer lives are dry and meaningless, and therefore, they don't get much out of it. Others have said that they don't have time to pray because they are too busy with family, work, prayer, and social activities.

A friend recently told me that God has not answered his prayers, so he gave up. Another said that she prayed for her son's recovery from a major illness, and he was not cured, so she won't pray anymore. Others, however, say that they have a very fruitful prayer life that gives them great joy and peace as well as daily guidance and direction from our Lord.

In reality, prayer is not optional if we want to have a life of happiness and holiness. It is a requirement handed down to us directly from our Lord Jesus Christ. He gave us many examples of how to pray which have been recorded in the Gospels. In John's Gospel, Jesus engages in spontaneous prayer, asking the Father to protect His disciples so that no soul gets lost, to bless His followers with the same joy that He experiences, to keep them from all temptations from the evil one, to consecrate them in the truth of God's ways, to guide them in proclaiming the good news, and to bless all those who receive the good news (John 17:1, 9, 11–21).

In Luke's Gospel, Jesus tells the apostles how to pray to His Father. He says to them, "When you pray, say: Father, hallowed be Your name, Your kingdom come. Give us each day our daily bread and forgive us our sins for we ourselves forgive everyone in debt to us, and do not subject us to the final test" (Luke 11:1–4). Jesus even prayed spontaneously to His Father for those who tortured Him while He was dying on the Cross, saying, "Father, forgive them, they know not what they do" (Luke 23:34).

Through her many apparitions around the world, our Blessed Mother Mary has told us to pray frequently each day in order to stay focused on God's will. St. Paul tells us to, "Pray without ceasing" (1 Thess. 5:17). St. Thérèse Couderc lived in the 1800s and founded the order of the Sisters of the Cenacle. She said this about prayer:

> Oh, if people could just understand ahead of time the sweetness and peace that are savored when nothing is held back from the good God! How He communicates to the one who seeks Him sincerely and has known how to surrender himself. Let them experience it, and they will see that here is found the true happiness they are vainly seeking elsewhere.[27]

---

[27] Cenacle Sisters, The Cenacle Newsletter of the Metairie Cenacle Retreat House, Summer 2015.

The elements of a strong prayer life are very simple:

Be humble of heart with no expectation. Jesus praised a tax collector who humbled himself in prayer saying, "O God, be merciful to me a sinner." By contrast, our Lord criticized the Pharisee who exalted himself praying, "O God, I thank you that I am not like the rest of humanity — greedy, dishonest, adulterous — or even like this tax collector. I fast twice a week, and I pay tithes on my whole income." Jesus further told us, "For everyone who exalts himself will be humbled, and the one who humbles himself will be exalted" (Luke 18:11–14).

Be patient. Our Lord responds in His time and not ours. We often want an immediate response to our prayers, and if He doesn't respond right away, we give up and think He isn't listening. Rest assured that God is never on vacation nor out of the office. He is listening to us all the time. "Be still before the LORD; wait for God" (Ps. 37:7).

Be persistent. Exodus describes a war between Amalek and Israel. Moses was the leader of Israel at the time. During the war, as long as Moses was praying with his hands raised, the Israelites were winning the war. If he stopped praying and lowered his hands, his people began to lose. Moses was persistent and kept praying with his hands raised with the help of Aaron and Hur, and the Israelites won the war (Exod. 17:8–13). St. Paul emphasizes persistence in prayer. In his Letter to the Romans, he says, "Persevere in prayer" (Rom. 12:12).

Have unwavering faith in His merciful love for us. Prayer sustains faith, which allows us to call on God day or night as necessary. "It is even the first and most natural way to express our faith" (Fr. Jacques Philippe).[28]

Be thankful to our Lord for listening to our prayers. Ten lepers came to Jesus and said, "Jesus, Master! Have pity on us" (Luke 17:14). Our Lord instructed them to present themselves to the priests. As they were traveling to see the priest, they were cured. But only one of them came back to thank our Lord. Jesus asked, "Ten were cleansed, were they not? Where are the other nine?" (Luke 17:17).

Our Lord wants us to be thankful for His response to our prayers. The *Catechism of the Catholic Church* describes prayer as communion with God. "Prayer is the living relationship of the children of God with their Father who is good beyond measure, with His Son Jesus Christ and with the Holy Spirit.... The life of prayer is the habit of being in the presence of the thrice-holy God and in communion with Him" (CCC 2565).

There are many ways to pray in order to have a strong prayer life. There is no one way that is better than another. Varying our form of prayer can prevent the common complaints of dryness, lack of time, dissatisfaction, and delay in a response from our Lord. The kinds of prayer to consider are as follows:

Pray for others each day. Pray for the deceased that have made a difference in your life, that they are in Heaven, and if not, pray that Jesus bless them with eternal life in accordance with His will. This list can include parents, family members, teachers, coaches, co-workers, friends,

---

[28] Fr. Jacques Philippe, *Thirsting for Prayer* (New Rochelle, NY: Scepter Publishers, 2014), 40.

and anyone else. St. Thomas Aquinas discussed praying for the souls in Purgatory. He said, "Of all prayers, the most acceptable to God are prayers for the dead, because they imply all the works of charity both corporal and spiritual."[29] Also, pray for your family, friends, or acquaintances who are suffering physically, psychologically, spiritually, or emotionally. Ask our Lord to bless these souls with a speedy recovery from their suffering so they can return to serve Him in the special mission He has for them. Further ask Him to bless them with the grace and peace to manage this time in their lives. Pray for your needs and guidance from Jesus to solve problems and make decisions. Bl. Pauline von Mallinckrodt was the foundress of the Sisters of Christian Charity. She described prayer to God this way: "Whatever the situation, talk it over with God, invoke His counsel, and receive His interior direction for your actions."[30]

Discuss your day with Jesus. Spend spiritual reflection time with Jesus just as you would spend time with your spouse or a close friend. Think of it as a daily examen of conscience as recommended by St. Ignatius of Loyola (Part II, Chapter 2).

Consider praying traditional rote prayers. We are all familiar with prayers such as the Our Father, Hail Mary, and Glory Be. Consider praying the Rosary daily, and meditating on the Joyful, Sorrowful, Glorious, or Luminous mysteries.

---

[29] PurgatoryPeople.com.

[30] Imprimatur: Most Reverend Frank J. Rodimer, Bishop of the Diocese of Paterson, NJ. February 26, 1988.

There are hundreds of other prayers to consider which can be accessed online or through free apps such as Laudate. There is a misconception that these prayers are dry and boring. St. Teresa of Avila describes what the soul gains from a perfect recitation of a rote prayer:

> To keep you from thinking that little is gained from perfect recitation of a rote prayer without distraction, it is very possible that while reciting the Our Father, the Lord may raise you to perfect contemplation. His Majesty shows that He listens to the one who speaks to Him. It is His grandeur that speaks to the soul, suspending one's intellect, binding one's imagination, taking the words from one's mouth.[31]

Try a prayerful reading of Scripture. This is one of the very best ways to pray, because our Lord truly speaks to those who study His ways. Consider reading one of the books of the Gospel from beginning to end, taking one chapter at a time. Follow the *Lectio Divina* message of Scripture review. This is a traditional Benedictine practice of scriptural analysis. The steps for this review are to read a passage of Scripture, meditate on its meaning, pray to our Lord in your own words, and contemplate ways we can be transformed by God's grace to do His will. Pope Benedict XVI wrote in his encyclical *Verbum Domini* about this form of prayer:

> We do well also to remember that the process of *lectio divina* is not concluded until it arrives at an

---

[31] St. Teresa of Avila, *The Way of Perfection*, chap. 25.

action, which moves the believer to make his or her life a gift for others in charity.[32]

Pray with others. One of the best ways to grow spiritually is to share our spiritual experiences with others. Meeting on a weekly or monthly basis with family members or friends to pray the Rosary together or do a Bible study helps each of us to learn from the thoughts of others. Sharing ideas in a small group on the ways our Lord is speaking to us can be very rewarding. Jesus tells us that, "For where two or three are gathered together in my name, there am I in the midst of them" (Matt. 18:20).

Consider keeping a personal journal. Spend time each day recording your reflections on the events of the day in a journal. Describe the issues that you face in your life. Reflect on your blessings from Jesus. Discern the path forward in service to God and others.

Don't hesitate to invoke the aid of Our Blessed Mother Mary and the saints. Study the life of Our Blessed Mother Mary. Pray to her to intercede to her Son, Jesus, for your prayer requests. Also, study the lives of the saints, as they are great role models for us. Remember St. Louis de Montfort and his great devotion to our Blessed Mother Mary. He is well known today because of his total consecration to Jesus through Mary. His prayer to Our Lady says in part, "Destroy in me all that may be displeasing to God, root it up, and bring it to naught.... Grant, if it be possible,

---

[32] Pope Benedict XVI, Apostolic Letter *Verbum Domini* (September 2010), no. 87.

that I may have no other spirit but thine; to know Jesus and His divine will.... To work zealously and unselfishly for thee until death as the humblest of thy servants."[33]

The fruits of a dedicated and focused prayer life are awesome. We can experience true joy and happiness, daily direction in all decision-making, the courage to handle adversity, unlimited graces, and self-discipline to avoid temptation. But most of all, the greatest fruit is the chance to be in Heaven with our Lord. Think of prayer as an investment of our time to keep our souls healthy. We have everything to gain and nothing to lose.

[33] St. Louis de Montfort, Prayer to Mary, in *The Secret of Mary* (Charlotte, NC: TAN Books, 2016).

Spiritual Treasures for Reflection

"Of all prayers, the most acceptable to God are prayers for the dead, because they imply all the works of charity both corporal and spiritual." (St. Thomas Aquinas)

"Whatever the situation, talk it over with God, invoke His counsel, and receive His interior direction for your actions." (Bl. Pauline von Mallinckrodt)

"For where two or three are gathered together in My name, there am I in the midst of them." (Matt. 18:20)

"Be still before the Lord; wait for Him." (Ps. 37:7)

Personal Notes of Reflection

_____

_____

_____

_____

_____

Chapter 24

Making Good Decisions

Remember the television game show *Let's Make a Deal?* The show began in the 1960s, was restarted in 2009, and continues to air on television today. During the show, contestants are offered something of value and have to make a decision whether to keep it or make a deal to exchange it for a different unknown item. If the contestants decide to exchange their items, they either get a much better prize, such as jewelry, a trip, or a new car, or they get snookered and receive something of little value, such as an old, broken-down car, a gag gift, or a live animal. One of the fun parts of the show is watching the contestants make their decisions. Making decisions is an example of our God-given free will. God is calling us to make good choices with the freedom He has given us.

Jesus teaches us the importance of making good decisions. Remember the parable of the rich man and Lazarus. The rich man spent his time accumulating wealth and enjoying it by dressing in the finest clothes and eating the best foods. He was self-centered, not sharing his wealth with the poor nor being a good role model for his five brothers. To the contrary, Lazarus, a poor man, accepted his poverty, disease, and suffering. He would gladly have eaten the scraps from the rich man's table. There were consequences for the decisions made by the rich man and by Lazarus. At the end of their lives, both men were judged by God for the choices they made while living on earth. Lazarus was rewarded with the grand prize of Heaven. The rich man was taken to the netherworld to live in a state of torment (Luke 16:19–31).

Our Lord gives us further direction about the importance of making good decisions. Jesus tells us that no one can serve two masters. We have to choose between serving God or serving ourselves (Luke 16:13). Our souls were created to be in perfect communion with God, so our task is to serve God and avoid self-indulgence.

St. Paul teaches us about making good decisions by using our free will. He tells us to pursue righteousness, devotion, faith, love, patience, and gentleness. Furthermore, he states that we are to compete well for the Faith, pursue eternal life, and keep God's commandments (1 Tim. 6:11–12, 14).

The book of Proverbs in the Old Testament provides great wisdom on these matters. Many of the writings in this book are attributed to King Solomon. We are instructed to look to the LORD for guidance in making decisions. It states, "Trust in the Lord with all your heart, on your own intelligence rely not; in all your ways be mindful of him, and he will make straight your paths" (Prov. 3:5–6).

Following a process can lead to good decisions. St. Ignatius of Loyola developed the following Spiritual Exercises for decision making:

> *Pray.* Recognize God's presence in all that you do. When you pray regularly, you will easily be able to approach God for help in making a difficult choice, even when you must do so at the spur of the moment.

Look at all sides of the issue. Make a list of pros and cons. Weigh each side. You need to consider what people who you respect would say about this choice. Also consider what the Church has to say.

Imagine your final decision. Think about the consequences if you choose the way you think you will.... If you are uncomfortable ... you may be about to make a wrong choice.

Make your choice and act. If you have done the previous three steps, trust that God is helping you make the right choice. Act on what you have decided.

Evaluate your choice. If you later feel a sense of satisfaction after you have acted on your choice, you have likely made a good choice. Ask yourself if your relationship with God and others has improved or worsened because of the choice you made.[34]

During our lifetime, we have the freedom to make thousands of decisions. Some of them are simple and others are complex. The simple choices are the clothes we wear or the food we eat. The complex decisions can include where to live, which job to take, or whom to marry.

Sometimes, our selfish ways can cloud our thinking, and we can make bad choices. Early in my law practice, we represented physicians and hospitals in medical malpractice cases. In one of these cases, we had an expert obstetrician who told us about the choice one of his patients had to make. This patient had

---

[34] St. Ignatius of Loyola, *Engaging Faith: St. Ignatius of Loyola and Making Good Decisions* (Notre Dame, IN: Ave Maria Press, 2008).

three children and was early in her pregnancy with twins. The patient told our expert that she didn't think she could care for twins and wanted to abort one of them. When faced with this situation, the wise doctor showed the patient the ultrasound images of the twins and asked her which one she wanted to kill. The mother immediately burst into tears, realizing her selfish thinking was leading her to a horrible decision. She apologized for even thinking about an abortion.

It is important to examine how we choose to spend our time in a typical twenty-four-hour day. Most of us sleep for seven to eight hours, which accounts for one third of the day. During our work time, are we following Jesus' best practices of acting morally and ethically and treating others fairly? During our home time, are we totally consumed by entertainment, such as television, social media, or the phone? Have we carved out time to have dinner with our family? Do we set aside time for prayer, talking with Jesus, and spiritual reading? Organizing each day can help us stay on the path of making the choices that God wants.

Furthermore, we need to examine the activities we choose to be involved in. What are we doing to give back to Jesus for His blessings? Aside from going to Mass on the weekend, are we spending time directly in service to our Lord in one of His ministries, participating in a community activity or helping in our families? Even if we only have a few hours per month, there is a ministry for each of us. Consider this expression: Ask not what God can do for you but what you can do for God.

Ultimately, we have to answer to our Lord for the decisions we make in our lifetime. The prophet Amos addresses the issue this way: he says woe to those living lives of luxury, only thinking of themselves without caring for others, for "they shall be the first to go into exile" (Amos 6:7).

Think about it this way. We are all contestants in the game show of life. We can't afford to take the risk of deciding to serve ourselves over the choice to serve God. We don't want to get "snookered" by bad choices and be given an eternity of torment in the netherworld. Rather, we want to be rewarded with the grand prize of Heaven. Eventually, our time on this earth will expire, and we will no longer have the opportunity to make any further decisions. You see, this matter of choice is serious business. Make good decisions now and every day, as this may be our last day to choose to serve God. We can't live for ourselves today and ignore the consequences of tomorrow.

Spiritual Treasures for Reflection

"No servant can serve two masters. He will either hate one and love the other, or be devoted to one and despise the other. You cannot serve God and mammon." (Luke 16:13)

"Trust in the Lord with all your heart, on your own intelligence rely not; in all your ways be mindful of him, and he will make straight your paths." (Prov. 3:5–6)

Personal Notes of Reflection

_____

_____

_____

_____

_____

Chapter 25

Spread the Good News

When our son Grant was four years old, my wife Rosalyn gave him instructions to get dressed and pick up his toys. Grant replied with an unexpected response. It was not: "Sure, Mom, I would be glad to do it." Instead, he said, "You are not the boss of me." As she maintained control, fighting back laughter, Rosalyn set Grant straight about who was the boss.

All of us have been on the receiving end of instructions. They can come from teachers, bosses, parents, or coaches. Teachers instruct students about academic requirements, discipline policies, and classroom etiquette. Our bosses tell us to do certain projects, contact specific accounts, and do administrative tasks. Children learn about homework rules, curfews, and behavior expectations from their parents. Coach Sean Payton of the New Orleans Saints tells his players to "do your job."

In Matthew's Gospel, Jesus instructs the apostles about ways to spread the good news and about how we should live. Our Lord gives these instructions because He wants every soul to experience the great joys of this life and the rewards of eternal life.

In one of His instructions, Jesus says, "Behold, I am sending you like sheep in the midst of wolves; so be shrewd as serpents and simple as doves" (Matt. 10:16). Furthermore, He says, "Therefore do not be afraid of them" (Matt. 10:26). Our Lord implores us to let no one intimidate us nor cause us to back down from our beliefs. He wants us to stay focused on the specific mission He has for each of us to spread the good news.

A second instruction to us from our Lord concerns standing up for our beliefs when they are challenged. Jesus tells us not to worry nor to think twice about taking a stand. "Do not worry about how you are to speak or what you are to say. You will be given at that moment what you are to say. For it will not be you who speak but the Spirit of your Father speaking through you" (Matt. 10:19–20).

We can't be afraid to stand up to others concerning our faith, including on issues such as the right to life, importance of Mass on Sundays, sacraments, daily prayer, and teachings of the Church. Don't be hesitant to challenge others in a reasonable way as to their beliefs that are counter to our faith. St. Paul tells us, "Say these things. Exhort and correct with all authority. Let no one look down on you" (Titus 2:15).

In the world today, there are all kinds of nonbelievers who try to dissuade us from our Christian values. They promote illicit and immoral ways. Many in the news media, politics, and Hollywood try to reshape us, control our opinions, and rob us of our joy in life. "Fake news" is generated to foster violence, fear, and hatred of others. Some promote the recreational use of illegal drugs, excessive consumption of alcohol, and disorderly conduct as cool, and immoral sex as a sport. There is no respect for human life, especially the unborn and the elderly.

To overcome this assault on our Christian values, we must be courageous. The opposite of fear is courage, which is one of the gifts of the Holy Spirit (Isa. 11:2). It is the antidote for worry and fear. Courage evokes determination and drive to fulfill our

Lord's mission that He has for each one of us. Is our individual mission in today's world any less important than the apostles' mission two thousand years ago? The times may be different, but the challenges and opportunities are the same.

A third instruction to us from our Lord is to shout the good news from the housetops. Jesus says, "What I say to you in the darkness, speak in the light; what you hear whispered, proclaim on the housetops" (Matt. 10:27). How are we to respond to God's call to spread the good news two thousand years after Jesus asked His apostles to do this? St. Paul tells us that in God's plan of salvation, we were chosen before the foundation of the world to be holy and without blemish before Him (Eph. 1:4).

From the time we wake up in the morning until we close our eyes at night, we should be spreading the good news. Our Lord's values have to be at the center of all that we think, do, and say. This action begins with the way we treat our family members at home before we leave for the day. We can't drop the ball at home before we go out in public. This godly mindset must continue throughout the day in all our communication with others, whether it be personal interaction or by emails, text messages, tweets, or Instagram posts. All our communications have to reflect our core Christian values. Think about it this way: Can we really expect to be a positive influence on others if we are not carrying the torch for our Lord in all that we do?

We can spread our Lord's ways by doing small things in our daily service to others. How about doing chores around the house that we don't usually do, such as cooking or cleaning? Perhaps we can donate an hour or two of our time to help a disabled neighbor who is struggling and has great needs. Surely, there are occasions when we can help a co-worker who needs assistance on a project. Giving some of our time to visit a sick friend or family member is excellent. Think about writing a note or a letter to someone who needs encouragement. Daily prayer is so valuable for those who have great needs and are suffering. By our actions, others will see Jesus at work in us and will want to imitate Him.

Ministry work in our parishes is worth considering as well. Each parish has numerous ministries to choose from, such as bringing the Eucharist to the homebound or to those in nursing homes and hospitals, cooking meals for a homeless shelter, serving at Mass, participating in a faith-based organization such as the Knights of Columbus or St. Vincent de Paul Society, teaching religious education, or volunteering in the parish office. The needs are great, but the workers are few.

Whether we like it or not, each one of us is under a microscope. Others are watching our actions and listening to our words. We have to be positive role models, especially when we are around children, whose watchful eyes are fixed on their parents and grandparents. If parents curse or use racial slurs, children will think it is okay to say those things too.

Similarly, managers are carefully watched by those they supervise. If the manager breaks the company policy of not using social media during the workday, then the employees will do the same. By contrast, if they see the manager going out of his way to assist his workers, they will do likewise for their co-workers. They will view it as a team effort.

The saints are great role models who followed Jesus' instructions to spread the good news. Remember the story of St. Mother Théodore Guerin, of the Sisters of Providence, who answered God's call. She went to southern Indiana from France in the 1850s to start a Catholic school system from scratch. St. Mother Théodore had very few resources and had to rely on the providence of God for money, people to build the schools, and parents to recognize the importance of giving their children a Catholic education. St. Mother Théodore started more than a dozen schools in Indiana.

Bl. Miguel Pro was a Jesuit priest who lived in Mexico in the mid-1920s. At the time, the Mexican government had closed all the churches and forced Catholics to go underground. Despite the actions of the government, Bl. Miguel Pro continued to serve as a priest by celebrating Mass and helping the poor by providing them with clothes and medical supplies. He would not be deterred from spreading the good news despite the oppression of the Mexican government. For his efforts to practice his faith as a priest, Bl. Miguel Pro was arrested and later executed for a false crime. At the time of his execution by firing squad, he faced his executioners with a crucifix in one hand, a rosary in the other and holding his arms out in imitation of the Crucifixion of our Lord. During his execution, he shouted, *"¡Viva Cristo Rey!"* which means, "Long live Christ the King!"[35]

Our Lord tells us about the grand prize that is waiting for us if we follow His instructions to spread the good news. He says, "Everyone who acknowledges me before others I will acknowledge before my heavenly Father" (Matt. 10:32). The reward is Heaven.

---

[35] Deacon Brian Wentz, "Viva Cristo Rey," *Wait . . . So That's What Catholics Believe?!?!* (blog), November 25, 2012.

Spiritual Treasures for Reflection

"Behold, I am sending you like sheep in the midst of wolves; so be shrewd as serpents and simple as doves.... Therefore do not be afraid of them." (Matt. 10:16, 26)

"Do not worry about how you are to speak or what you are to say. You will be given at that moment what you are to say. For it will not be you who speak but the Spirit of your Father speaking through you." (Matt. 10:19–20)

"What I say to you in the darkness, speak in the light; what you hear whispered, proclaim on the housetops." (Matt. 10:27)

"Everyone who acknowledges me before others I will acknowledge before my heavenly Father." (Matt. 10:32)

Personal Notes of Reflection

_____

_____

_____

_____

_____

Chapter 26

Guardian Angels Are
at Work in Your Life

The archangel Gabriel was part of one of the greatest events in the history of the world. He was sent by God to ask Mary if she would be the Mother of Jesus. Gabriel explained to Mary that by the power of the Holy Spirit, she would conceive a baby who was the Son of God (Luke 1:26–35). Mary humbly said yes to God's request from Gabriel. As mentioned previously, she spoke these famous words: "Behold, I am the handmaid of the Lord. May it be done to me according to your Word" (Luke 1:38). Angels such as Gabriel perform a major role in God's mission for His people on earth. Sadly, they are often ignored by us. It is important to recognize that angels are at work in our lives. They are here to help us get to Heaven.

The *Catechism of the Catholic Church* describes angels as servants and messengers of God. They serve God's salvation plan for us and do His work (CCC 328, 329, 331). "Angels have intelligence and will: they are personal and immortal creatures, surpassing in perfection all visible creatures" (CCC 330). The angels surround Christ their Lord and were created for and through Him (CCC 331). "Angels have been present since creation and throughout the history of salvation" (CCC 332).

Angels were there for Jesus when He was born (Luke 2:9–14). They aided Him in the desert when He was tempted by the devil (Matt. 4:1–11). An angel helped strengthen Jesus when He was in agony in the garden before His Crucifixion (Luke 22:39–46).

According to Holy Scripture, there are different types of angels, including archangels, cherubim, seraphim, and guardian angels. Archangels get direct assignments from God to do things on earth, and there are at least three of them: Michael, Raphael and Gabriel. Michael is a mighty warrior who leads God's army against Satan (Rev. 12:7). Raphael is the angel of healing because he delivered Tobit from blindness (Tob. 11:1–14). Gabriel announced God's plan to Mary (Luke 1:26–35). The angels known as cherubim are in God's presence (Ezek. 10:1–8). The seraphim are around the throne of God and praise Him (Isa. 6:1–3).

We also need to recognize that we each have a guardian angel assigned to us. Recall the experience of St. Padre Pio. When he was a boy, his guardian angel appeared to him and became his companion for life. On one occasion, this great saint told his confessor about his guardian angel. To test Padre Pio about his spiritual friend, the confessor wrote Padre Pio a letter in Greek and asked him to translate it. This was a language that the saint did not know. Padre Pio returned the letter to the confessor translated from Greek to English. The confessor asked him how he was able to do it, and his response was that his guardian angel helped him. Later, Padre Pio wrote using foreign languages even though he never studied them. His knowledge came from his guardian angel. This very special saint often wrote letters to friends, encouraging them to recognize that their guardian angels were always with them.

The *Catechism of the Catholic Church* describes guardian angels this way: "From its beginning until death, human life is surrounded by their watchful care and intercession. 'Beside each believer stands an angel as protector and shepherd leading him to life.' Already here on earth the Christian life shares by faith in the blessed company of angels and men united in God" (CCC 336). Jesus explains that the work of guardian angels is to serve as caretakers for each individual soul. He says, "See that you do not despise one of these little ones, for I say to you that their angels in heaven always look upon the face of my heavenly Father" (Matt. 18:10).

In the Old Testament book of Tobit, there is a story about the role of a guardian angel. The son of Tobit was leaving on a long journey. His mother was concerned about his safety. Tobit reassured his wife that their son would be safe because his guardian angel would be with him. Tobit told his wife, "For a good angel will go with him, his journey will be successful, and he will return unharmed" (Tob. 5:17–22).

Guardian angels have made their presence known in recent times. My mother, Mary Eason, was told by her doctor that she had terminal cancer and only had a few months to live. Mom had great peace all through the dying process. One night when I was talking with her, she told me that her guardian angel was communicating with her. She further explained that the name of her guardian angel was spelled Meri, which was slightly different from the spelling of her own name. Her guardian angel, Meri, comforted her all during her suffering.

Ashley Code, the sixteen-year-old student at Mount Carmel Academy who was diagnosed with a brain tumor, also encountered her guardian angel. One night, after a biopsy of the tumor, Ashley was at home lying in bed with her mother with only candlelight in the room. Ashley told her mother, "Our guardian angels are in the room with us. Jesus is in the room, too. Jesus said don't be scared, Mom." Ashley fought brain cancer for more than a year before she passed away. She drew great comfort from her guardian angel during her suffering.

There is a prayer to guardian angels to solicit their help: "Angel of God, my guardian dear, to whom God's love commits me here. Ever this day be at my side, to light and guard, to rule and guide. Amen." Make no mistake about it. Guardian angels are real. As Jesus encouraged us, take the time to recognize your guardian angel working in your life. God put these angels here to help us in our journey through life.

Spiritual Treasures for Reflection

"Beside each believer stands an angel as protector and shepherd leading him to life." (CCC 336)

"For I say to you that their angels in heaven always look upon the face of My heavenly Father." (Matt. 18:10)

"For a good angel will go with him, his journey will be successful, and he will return unharmed." (Tob. 5:22)

Personal Notes of Reflection

_____

_____

_____

_____

_____

Chapter 27

Saints Are Awesome Intercessors and Spiritual Mentors for Us

Who are the saints? They are special souls who lived exemplary lives on earth. Routinely, they practiced the theological virtues of faith, hope, and charity and the cardinal virtues of prudence, fortitude, courage, and justice. All of them were close to God, and they brought others closer to Him.

Studying the life of a saint is most rewarding. Many were raised in devout households where the Catholic faith was practiced. Others came from dysfunctional families and learned to know Jesus and His ways through mentors. Some of them lived separate and apart from our Lord for a time and later changed their ways based on a spontaneous event. Others evolved into living a saintly life over time. All of them have in common the complete surrender of their souls to the will of Jesus; they left their earthly ways behind. They are known for their intense devotion to Jesus and His values.

Becoming a saint is not based on living a long life. Some only lived for a short time, and others until old age. St. Thérèse of Lisieux lived to age twenty-four. St. Maria Faustina Kowalska died at age thirty-three. St. Padre Pio was called home to Heaven when he was eighty-one years old. St. Teresa of Calcutta passed away at age eighty-seven. Recognition as a saint is based on living a sustained period of time devoted totally to the will of our Lord and His ways of holiness.

There are four stages in the canonization process for a person to become a saint. The process can only begin five years from the date of death of the individual. In stage one, a formal request is made by any Catholic or group of Catholics to the local bishop of the diocese where the person died. The request must describe the life of holiness demonstrated by the candidate and identify the reasons for sainthood. If the local bishop finds there is the required amount of evidence, he can make a request to the Vatican for the opportunity to open a local tribunal to investigate the life of the person. The tribunal calls witnesses to testify to the candidate's life of devotion to God, dedication to virtue, and holiness. Affidavits based on the personal knowledge of witnesses of the candidate are often gathered. A person who completes stage one is named a "Servant of God."

In stage two, the local bishop sends a formal report and request to the Vatican for consideration of the candidate for sainthood by the Congregation for the Causes of Saints. This body appoints a relator. A position paper is drafted describing the virtues of the Servant of God and may be very lengthy. The congregation votes on the cause, and if the vote is unanimous, the candidate moves on to the pope for his consideration. Once approved by the pontiff, the person is designated as "venerable."

The third stage is beatification. Candidates who died for their faith are referred to as martyrs and can be beatified on this basis. For all others to be considered for this stage, there must be a miracle arising from the intercession of the person to Jesus. This miracle must be confirmed by the Congregation of the Causes of Saints. Upon approval by the congregation, the person is beatified and called "blessed." Once this designation is made, the blessed can be venerated by others.

The final stage is canonization. To reach this stage, a second miracle attributable to the intercessory efforts of the candidate to Jesus is necessary. Again, the miracle must be approved by the congregation. After approval, the prefect of the congregation forwards the candidate to the pope for final decision. Once the pontiff accepts the candidate, a Mass of canonization occurs to honor the new saint.

Everyone in the Church can benefit from developing a great relationship with the saints, because they can intercede to Jesus for our prayer requests and serve as mentors as to how to live a life of holiness.

The role of saints as intercessors requesting miracles from Jesus was established in our Lord's message to his disciples at the Last Supper:

> Believe me that I am in the Father and the Father is in me, or else, believe because of the works themselves. Amen, amen, I say to you, whoever believes in me will do the works that I do, and will do greater ones than these, because I am going to the Father. And whatever you ask in my name, I will do, so that the Father may be glorified in the Son. If you ask anything of me in my name, I will do it. (John 14:11–14)

The types of miracles attributable to the saints include healings, cures, the stigmata, prophecy, and experiencing voices from Heaven. Even the bodies of several of the saints remain incorrupt after death.

One of the miracles attributed to St. Teresa of Calcutta involved the healing of an Indian woman, Monica Besra. She had an abdominal tumor, and her physicians abandoned hope of saving her life. She was taken to the Missionaries of Charity, but her health continued to decline. On the one-year anniversary of the passing of Mother Teresa, one of the sisters placed a Miraculous Medal that had been touched by the saint on the abdomen of the Indian patient. She fell asleep, and when she woke up, the pain was gone. A subsequent evaluation by the attending physicians indicated that the tumor was gone.

In the summer of 1919, an elderly handicapped man, Francisco Santarello, was the beneficiary of a miracle cure through St. Padre Pio. Mr. Santarello had a severe club foot which prevented him from walking. He was only able to get around on his knees, supported by small crutches. One day, he was near the door of the residence of St. Padre Pio, begging for alms. As the saint exited his residence on the way to church for Mass, Mr. Santarello asked the saint to give him a blessing. The response from the saint was: "Throw away your crutches!" Thereafter, Mr. Santarello threw down his crutches and walked away. The miracle cure was witnessed by dozens of people and reported in the local newspaper.[36]

St. Anthony Mary Claret, who lived in the 1800s, was approached by José and Rosa Malato about the desire of their daughter, Candida, to enter the religious life. The parents were reluctant to agree to this request, as Candida was their only child. St. Anthony prophesied that within one year, God would grant them a son, which would allow them to give their daughter permission to join the Carmelite order. The father was very doubtful of the prophecy from the saint, as his wife was well past childbearing age.

---

[36] MiraclesoftheSaints.com.

One year to the day, a son was born to the Malatos. Thereafter, Candida joined the Carmelite order.[37]

St. Padre Pio was given the wounds of Christ, the stigmata, when Jesus and Mary appeared to him on September 7, 1910. He experienced the invisible stigmata almost weekly for a few years. In 1918, the saint had a vision of Jesus and was given the visible stigmata on his hands, feet, and side. He suffered from the stigmata throughout the rest of his life until his death on September 23, 1968.

The saints are awesome spiritual mentors because of the way they lived their lives and because of their written works. Some of the best-known writings of these special souls come from St. Thérèse of Lisieux, St. Maria Faustina Kowalska, St. Teresa of Calcutta, and St. Padre Pio.

In 1895, St. Thérèse was ordered by Reverend Mother Agnes, the prioress of the Carmel order, to write about her childhood memories. Some of the written messages from St. Thérèse were about how to become a saint, focusing on doing the will of Jesus, overcoming fear, and managing suffering. She wrote, "I understand that to become a saint, one has to suffer much, seek out always the most perfect thing to do, and forget self." As mentioned before, she further wrote, "My God, I choose all. I don't want to be a saint by halves. I'm not afraid to suffer for You, I fear only one thing: to keep my own will. So take it, for I choose all that You will." Another thought from this saint states, "Souls in the state of grace have nothing to fear." Also, she wrote, "How good God really is! How He parcels out trials only according to the strength He gives us."[38]

---

[37] MiraclesoftheSaints.com.
[38] *Story of a Soul*, 27.

St. Maria Faustina Kowalska described in her diary the apparitions that she had with our Lord. During one of them, she was given a message about proclaiming Jesus' mercy for all mankind. Our Lord told her, "Make known to souls the great mercy that I have for them, and exhort them to trust in the bottomless depth of My mercy." Then, on February 22, 1931, Jesus appeared to the saint again. She wrote about having trust in our Lord:

> In the evening, when I was in my cell, I became aware of the Lord Jesus clothed in a white garment. One hand was raised in blessing, the other was touching the garment at the breast. From the opening of the garment at the breast there came forth two large rays, one red and the other pale. In silence I gazed intently at the Lord; my soul was overwhelmed with fear, but also with great joy. After a while Jesus said to me, "Paint an image according to the pattern you see, with the inscription: Jesus, I trust in You."[39]

St. Teresa of Calcutta described the proper measure of helping others as giving until it hurts. She said, "We must grow in love, and to do this we must go on loving and loving and giving and giving until it hurts, the way Jesus did. Do ordinary things with extraordinary love: little things like caring for the sick and the homeless, the lonely and the unwanted, washing and cleaning for them. You must give what will cost you something."[40]

St. Padre Pio described the importance of the continued presence of Jesus in our lives in a prayer known as "Stay with Me, Lord." Here are some parts of the prayer:

[39] *Diary*, no. 47.
[40] Maalouf, *Mother Teresa: Essential Writings*.

Stay with me, Lord, for it is necessary to have You present so that I do not forget You. You know how easily I abandon You. Stay with me, Lord, because I am weak and I need Your strength, that I may not fall so often. Stay with me, Lord, for You are my life, and without You, I am without meaning and hope.... Stay with me, Lord, to show me Your will. Stay with me, Lord, so that I can hear Your voice and follow You.... Grant that I may love You with all my heart while on earth, so that I can continue to love You perfectly throughout all eternity, dear Jesus, Amen![41]

Wow! It is truly a great joy to spend time studying the lives of the saints. Those mentioned here are typical of all the individuals who have been canonized over the centuries. We should be inspired by their holy lives as we seek to pursue the virtues they manifested to the world. These women and men lived on earth just like us. We have the same opportunity each day to follow their lead in working to get to Heaven, replacing our will with the will of Jesus and imitating His ways. They are in Heaven to serve as our intercessors and as our spiritual mentors. And so we ask them to pray for us, that we may someday join them in Heaven as fellow saints and serve as intercessors and mentors for others.

---

[41] St. Padre Pio, "Stay with Me, Lord," Capuchinfriars.org.

Spiritual Treasures for Reflection

"My God, I choose all. I don't want to be a saint by halves. I'm not afraid to suffer for You, I fear only one thing: to keep my own will. So take it, for I choose all that you will." (St. Thérèse of Lisieux)

"Make known to souls the great mercy that I have for them, and to exhort them to trust in the bottomless depth of My mercy." (St. Maria Faustina Kowalska)

"We must grow in love, and to do this we must go on loving and loving and giving and giving until it hurts, the way Jesus did. Do ordinary things with extraordinary love: little things like caring for the sick and the homeless, the lonely and the unwanted." (St. Mother Teresa of Calcutta)

Personal Notes of Reflection

_____

_____

_____

_____

_____

Chapter 28

Heaven Is Real

There is a basic bedrock set of principles or codes that exist for many types of jobs in the U.S. economy. For engineers, there are principles of momentum, resistance, force, and energy. These concepts impact the design of materials and products. Attorneys must follow codes of law that apply to business transactions, litigation, and family matters. For information technology specialists, there are principles that apply to the design and development of hardware and software that are used to create computers. Construction contractors are required to design and construct homes, buildings, and roads according to various applicable building codes.

Through the Transfiguration of Jesus on Mount Tabor, several basic bedrock principles of our faith were established. One is that the Holy Trinity is real. Secondly, Heaven offers us eternal happiness with God, Jesus, the Holy Spirit, our Blessed Mother Mary, the angels, and the saints. The Synoptic Gospels of Matthew, Mark, and Luke describe the events of the Transfiguration (Matt. 17:1–8, Mark 9:2–8, Luke 9:28–36). During the Transfiguration, Jesus turned into His divine self in the presence of the apostles

Peter, James, and John. The Holy Spirit, Moses, and Elijah were present, and God spoke to these apostles from Heaven.

From the Transfiguration, we learn that Jesus, God, and the Holy Spirit are not fictional characters. They truly exist as divine beings and are members of the Holy Trinity. Peter, James, and John experience supernatural events as proof of the existence of the Holy Trinity. During this event, the face of Jesus shone like the sun, His clothes were dazzling white, and our Lord was conversing with Moses and Elijah. Jesus demonstrated His true divinity to these apostles. God spoke to Jesus and the three apostles, saying: "This is my beloved Son, with whom I am well pleased; listen to him" (Matt. 17:5). The Holy Spirit was present with God in a shining cloud (CCC 555).

This supernatural event on Mount Tabor confirmed that Heaven is a real place. Moses and Elijah lived hundreds of years before Jesus' time on earth. Moses was a great lawgiver, prophet, and leader of the Jewish people, and Elijah was a great prophet of his time. During the Transfiguration, Jesus spoke to Moses and Elijah in the presence of the apostles. Both of these prophets had died centuries earlier. The only place that this conversation could have taken place was in Heaven. Also, clearly the voice from the cloud was from God in Heaven. This event removed all doubts about the existence of Heaven.

Despite the Transfiguration, there is much speculation in the secular world about whether Heaven truly exists. It is often the subject of jokes. Heaven is sometimes described as a place in the clouds where chubby little angels with harps fly around, comforting others. Those who have doubts are robbing themselves of the great peace that comes with the faith that Heaven exists. St. Paul, in his Letter to the Colossians, further tells us about the existence of Heaven. He says, "If then you were raised with

Christ, seek what is above, where Christ is seated at the right hand of God. Think of what is above, not of what is on earth" (Col. 3:1–2).

The book of Revelation describes Heaven:

> These are the ones who have survived the time of
>> great distress; they have washed their robes and
>> made them white in the blood of the Lamb.
> For this reason they stand before God's throne
> and worship him day and night in his temple.
> The one who sits on the throne will shelter them.
> They will not hunger or thirst anymore, nor will
>> the sun or any heat strike them.
> For the Lamb who is in the center of the throne
>> will shepherd them and lead them to springs of
>> life-giving water,
> and God will wipe away every tear from their eyes.
>> (Rev. 7:14–17)

St. Maria Faustina Kowalska, a mystic of the Church, received numerous spiritual messages from our Lord and Our Blessed Mother Mary. She recorded in her diary her spiritual travels to both Heaven and Hell. This is what she recorded about Heaven:

> Today I was in heaven, in spirit, and I saw its unconceivable beauties and the happiness that awaits us after death. I saw how all creatures give ceaseless praise and glory to God. I saw how great is happiness in God, which spreads to all creatures, making them happy; and then all the glory and praise which springs from this happiness returns to its source; and they enter into the depths of God, contemplating the inner life of God, the Father, the Son,

and the Holy Spirit, whom they will never comprehend or fathom. This source of happiness is unchanging in its essence, but it is always new, gushing forth happiness for all creatures.[42]

So now that we know that Heaven is real, how do we get there? Jesus tells us the answer to this question. He instructs us to follow Him, as He is the Way, the Truth, and the Life. He further says that no one goes to God except through Him (John 14:6).

There are many earthly paths that we can take during our life. Some of these earthly roads lead to power, material things, or wealth. Some paths require trampling over others along the way or giving up Christian values. But there is only one simple path to Heaven. That road requires doing what Jesus teaches us through His Gospels. His way and His works are the truth. Each day, we have a choice to make as to which path to follow—the one reaping earthly benefits or the one producing the reward of Heaven. When Jesus says He is the Life, He is referring to His power to grant eternal life. St. Peter said to Jesus, "Master, to whom shall we go? You have the words of eternal life. We have come to believe and are convinced that You are the Holy One of God" (John 6:68–69).

Most importantly, our Lord Himself tells us that He has prepared a special place for us in Heaven. Jesus told the apostles these words at the Last Supper: "In my Father's house there are many dwelling places. If there were not, would I have told you that I am going to prepare a place for you? And if I go and prepare a place for you, I will come back again and take you to myself, so that where I am you also may be" (John 14:2–3).

[42] *Diary*, no. 777.

It is time for all of us to fully recognize that God has prepared a place for each one of us in Heaven. Furthermore, Jesus is the Way, the Truth, and the Life, and we can only get to Heaven by following Him and doing His ways.

Spiritual Treasures for Reflection

"If then you were raised with Christ, seek what is above, where Christ is seated at the right hand of God. Think of what is above, not of what is on earth." (Col. 3:1–2)

"Master, to whom shall we go? You have the words of eternal life. We have come to believe and are convinced that You are the Holy One of God." (John 6:68–69)

"In my Father's house there are many dwelling places. If there were not, would I have told you that I am going to prepare a place for you? And if I go and prepare a place for you, I will come back again and take you to Myself, so that where I am you also may be." (John 14:2–3)

Personal Notes of Reflection

_____

_____

_____

_____

_____

Part IV

An Individual Spiritual Plan of Excellence That Leads to a Life of Happiness, Holiness, and Heaven

Developing an Individual
Spiritual Plan (ISP) of Excellence

Businesses have a strategic plan to follow in order to achieve success. Sports teams create plans to win championships. And financial advisors create retirement plans for an individual's financial goals.

Each of these plans serve our earthly needs and enjoyment, which are only of value while we are in this life. They offer very little in shaping our spiritual lives. Our Lord is calling us to develop a different kind of plan to pursue spiritual excellence so that we will be ready for Heaven when He calls us from this world. He is asking us to develop an ISP.

In Matthew's Gospel, Jesus tells the parable of the foolish and the wise virgins and their preparation to meet their bridegroom. The five foolish virgins did not have oil for their lamps to light their way to the bridegroom. The five wise virgins were well prepared with all the oil they needed for their lamps. When the bridegroom came at midnight, only the wise virgins were admitted to the wedding feast (Matt. 25:1–13).

The oil that Jesus, the Bridegroom, refers to in the parable is good works that we need to do to be admitted to the wedding feast which is Heaven. Our Lord told this parable to His disciples as His Crucifixion was drawing near. He wanted to leave His apostles, disciples, and all of us with the important message that we must plan and be prepared for the day when we are called from this world.

So how do we develop an ISP? This plan has several components to consider:

Participate in the sacraments. This will keep us focused on Jesus. Attendance at Sunday Mass with reception of the Holy Eucharist is a must. Also consider attendance at daily Mass, if possible. Monthly Confession frees our souls from the burden of sin, gives us peace, and obtains mercy from our Lord for our transgressions. If you haven't been to Confession in a long time, just go.

Pray daily. There are excellent rote prayers such as the Our Father, the Rosary, the Chaplet of Divine Mercy, the Prayer to St. Michael the Archangel, and the litanies. Additionally, we need individual quality quiet time with God for reflection on the events of the day and to obtain guidance from Him. One way to do this is through adoration time alone with our Lord, preferably in a church or chapel. Also consider doing the Ignatian Examen by St. Ignatius of Loyola (pt. 2, chap. 2).

Quality family time. This is important, because it allows us to build and maintain strong relationships with our loved ones and to serve as role models. This time includes daily mealtime without distraction from cell phones or television, which allows the family to engage in meaningful dialogue. Prayer at bedtime is also essential for our children to nurture a relationship with Jesus.

Terminate sin. Identify one or two basic weaknesses and focus on eradicating these sinful ways that persecute our Lord and rob us of happiness and holiness in life.

Serve others. We need to help our family members and friends. Volunteering in a church ministry or in community activities to help the poor, marginalized, victimized, and children should be a priority. The simple question here is whether we are making a difference for others by serving them or if we are only helping ourselves.

Read spiritual material. This time will give our souls the nourishment needed to strengthen our Christian values. We have to feed our souls just like we feed our bodies in order to grow in our relationship with God. Since we often spend hours each day preparing and eating meals, why can't we spend ten to fifteen minutes each day feeding our souls?

Fasting leads to self-discipline. It gives us discipline and allows us to offer penance to God for our sinful ways. Discipline will help us fight against temptation and keep us focused on our Lord. We can fast not only from food but also from alcohol, television, social media, computers, cell phones, or anything else that we enjoy.

Give to charity. This component involves donation of resources. God has blessed us with abundant resources, so we need to share them with others to improve their lives.

The good news is that there are consultants to help us develop our ISP. They are all around us. The Holy Spirit will guide us in developing the various components of the plan. All we have to do is ask Him. St. Paul tells us that by the power of the Holy Spirit at work within us, we can accomplish far more than we can ask or imagine (Eph. 3:20).

Our Blessed Mother Mary has an abundance of grace to bestow on us, and she wants to give us all that we need to create and fulfill a spiritual plan to serve Jesus.

The saints and blessed are perfect role models for imitation—twenty-four of them are mentioned in this book. We need to study their lives.

The angels are there to give us messages from our Lord. Remember, St. Gabriel gave God's message to our Blessed Mother Mary when he said, "Hail, favored one! The Lord is with you" (Luke 1:28). Our guardian angels are also there to light, guard, rule, and guide us.

Priests, religious, deacons, and spiritual directors are available to meet with us to share ideas for ministry work, spirituality, and other activities

Developing an ISP will help us fulfill God's plan for us. St. Catherine of Siena said, "Be who God meant you to be and you will set the world on fire."[43]

We can't afford to procrastinate in developing an ISP. Don't put this task at the bottom of your to-do list. Put it at the top and make it a priority. It only takes twenty to thirty minutes in prayer to develop a quality plan that will guide us in our spiritual life. Perhaps you could find this time by giving up social media or television for just one night. Remember that Jesus taught us to be prepared; "Therefore, stay awake, for you know neither the day nor the hour" (Matt. 25:13).

[43] Merridith Frediani, "7 Quotes from St. Catherine of Siena," Ascension Press website, April 26, 2019.

Remember our Blessed Mother Mary, who so perfectly accepted God's plan for her: "Behold, I am the handmaid of the Lord. May it be done to me according to your word" (Luke 1:38). Her words offer us support and guidance in developing and pursuing our ISP.

The benefits of developing and executing an ISP are truly fantastic. There is no greater experience in this life than to know the feeling of divine peace, limitless joy, and holiness. We can achieve this by serving our Lord through His spiritual plan of excellence for us. Business and retirement plans are good for only a short time when we are in this world. However, pursuing spiritual excellence through execution of an ISP results in gaining Heaven.

Following is a sample ISP for guidance in drafting and executing your personal plan. Always remember that following your ISP is the path to happiness, holiness, and Heaven.

My Individual Spiritual Plan for Jesus
Remember, the rewards are heavenly!

Sacraments
Mass — how often: _____

Confession — how often: _____

Daily Prayer
Rote prayers (e.g., the Our Father, the Rosary, the Chaplet of Divine Mercy, and the St. Michael prayer) — when: _____

Reflection time with God, including the Ignatian Examen (part II, chapter 2) — when: _____

Adoration time — when: _____

Quality family time — when: _____

Termination of Sin
Identify one or two basic weaknesses to eliminate:

_____

Service to Others
Identify family, friends, ministry, and/or community activities:

_____

Spiritual Reading and Scripture Study
Suggested resources: *New American Bible*, Gospel of Matthew; *My Daily Bread* by Fr. Anthony Paone; *Resisting Happiness* by Matthew Kelly; *Heaven Starts Now* by Fr. John Riccardo; *Live Passionately* by Fr. Cedric Pisegna — when:_____

Fasting
Food, alcohol, TV, social media, computers, cell phones, other pleasures — what and when:_____

Charitable Giving
Share family resources with others

To whom:_____

Amount:_____

Part V

The Saints as Role Models
of Spiritual Excellence

Life of St. Thérèse of Lisieux

St. Thérèse was born on January 2, 1873, to her parents, Marie-Azélie Guérin Martin and Louis Martin. Her father was a watchmaker, and her mother was a lacemaker. They had nine children, but only five survived childbirth. St. Thérèse was the last child born in the family and grew up in the little town of Alençon, France.

The Martin family practiced their Catholic Faith by praying together, attending Mass, going on pilgrimages, and through fast and abstinence. The family helped abandoned children, the poor, and people who were dying.

Two sisters of the saint, Pauline and Marie, entered religious life at Lisieux Carmel. Before the age of fifteen, St. Thérèse approached the Carmelite order for permission to join but was denied. On November 20, 1887, she was in Rome with her father and spoke to Pope Leo XIII about obtaining his permission to enter the religious order. The pope told her that she would enter the order if God willed it. She was admitted to Carmel on April 9, 1888. Her assignments in the religious community were to work in the sacristy, paint pictures, write poems, clean the dining room, and instruct the novices.

Spiritual Excellence

In early 1895, St. Thérèse was ordered by Reverend Mother Agnes, the prioress of the Carmel order, to write about her childhood memories. Her memories contain many wonderful messages. She wrote, "I understand that to become a saint, one has to suffer much, seek out always the most perfect thing to do and forget self." Recall from above, she wrote, "My God, I choose all! I don't want to be a saint by halves. I'm not afraid to suffer for You, I fear only one thing: to keep my own will. So take it, for I choose all that You will." Another thought from this saint is, "A soul in the state of grace has nothing to fear." Also, she stated, "How good God really is! How He parcels out trials only according to the strength He gives us."

On January 20, 1896, St. Thérèse gave the book of her memories to Mother Agnes. The writings contained her "little way" of living life. She described herself as "a ball in the hands of the Child Jesus." A few months before her death, this saint said, "I feel that my mission is about to begin, my mission to make God loved as I love Him, to teach souls my little way." Her memories were produced into a book known as *Story of a Soul: The Autobiography of St. Thérèse of Lisieux*. Millions of copies of her book have been sold worldwide.

On May 17, 1925, St. Thérèse was canonized a saint by Pope Pius VI. The pope described her as the star of his pontificate. The canonization ceremony was in the presence of an audience of sixty thousand people in St. Peter's square. Later that evening, there were as many as five hundred thousand people there.

St. Thérèse is the patron saint of missions and florists.

Story of a Soul: The Autobiography of St. Thérèse of Lisieux, trans. John Clarke, O.C.D., 2nd ed. (Washington, DC: ICS Publications, 1976), viii, 27, 28, 47.

Life of St. Maria Faustina Kowalska

St. Maria Faustina Kowalska was born on August 25, 1905, to Stanislaus and Marianna Kowalska in Głogowiec, Poland. Her birth name was Helen. She was the third of ten children. Her father was a carpenter, and her family was poor and religious. As a child, Helen demonstrated a love of prayer, piety, and sensitivity to human misery. She only had three years of education, and at age sixteen, she became a housekeeper working in nearby cities to help her family.

At age eighteen, Helen had her first vision of the suffering Jesus. He asked her to become a religious. She approached many different orders but was rejected each time. Eventually, she was accepted into the convent of the Congregation of the Sisters of Our Lady of Mercy. After entering the convent, she received the name Sr. Maria Faustina of the Blessed Sacrament. Five years later, she made her perpetual vows of chastity, poverty, and obedience, thereby becoming a Sister of Mercy. Her primary duties in the order were as a cook, gardener, and doorkeeper. She was faithful to the rules of the order, was unselfish in her love of others, and was joyful.

St. Maria met with Fr. Michael Sopocko, who was the confessor to the nuns of the order. St. Maria told Fr. Sopocko about her conversations with Jesus. Initially, he questioned these conversations with Jesus but later encouraged her to keep a diary of them. The diary described extensive details of her spiritual life.

A review of her diary reveals the continuous efforts of St. Maria to be in union with God. She was blessed with many great graces, including contemplation, understanding of the Mercy of God, revelations, visions of Jesus, and prophecy. In her diary, St. Maria wrote about these many blessings given to her. "Neither graces, nor revelations, nor raptures, nor gifts granted to a soul make it perfect, but rather the intimate union of the soul with God. These gifts are merely ornaments of the soul but constitute neither its essence nor its perfection. My sanctity and perfection consist in the close union of my will with the will of God."

Our Lord and Savior Jesus assigned St. Maria the great mission of proclaiming His Mercy to all of mankind. He told her to "make known to souls the great Mercy that I have for them, and to exhort them to trust in the bottomless depth of My Mercy." Jesus further instructed her, "You are the secretary of My Mercy; I have chosen you for that office in this and the next life."

On February 22, 1931, Jesus visited St. Maria. She wrote in her diary:

> In the evening, when I was in my cell, I became aware of the Lord Jesus clothed in a white garment. One hand was raised in blessing, the other was touching the garment at the breast. From the opening of the garment at the breast there came forth two large rays, one red and the other pale. In silence I gazed intently at the Lord; my soul was overwhelmed with fear, but also with great joy. After a while Jesus said to me, "Paint an image according to the pattern you see, with the inscription: Jesus, I trust in You."

During the same message of February 22, 1931, Jesus told St. Maria that He wanted His image "to be solemnly blessed on the first Sunday after Easter; that Sunday is to be the Feast of Mercy."

St. Maria was called by our Lord from this life on October 5, 1938. The funeral was on the first Friday of the month on the feast of Our Lady of the Rosary. She was canonized in Rome by Pope St. John Paul II on April 30, 2000, on Divine Mercy Sunday. During the canonization homily, Pope St. John Paul II said that each year, the second Sunday of Easter will be called Divine Mercy Sunday.

St. Maria is the patron saint of Mercy.

Diary of Saint Maria Faustina Kowalska (Stockbridge, MA: Marian Press, 2012), nos. 47, 49, 1107, 1567, 1605.

Life of St. Teresa of Calcutta

St. Teresa was born on August 26, 1910, in Skopje, Albania. Her birth name was Anjezë Gonxhe Bojaxhiu. She was the youngest of three children. Her father was Nikollë Bojaxhiu. He was a building contractor. Her mother was Dranafile Bojaxhiu. After the early death of her husband, Mrs. Bojaxhiu started a business selling cloth and embroidery to support her family.

In her teenage years, St. Teresa became interested in missionary work through a ministry in her local church parish. At the age of eighteen, she had a calling to join the Sisters of Loreto. This religious order focused on missionary work in various countries, including India. After living with the order in Ireland, St. Teresa was assigned to work as a teacher at St. Mary's High School in Calcutta, India. On May 24, 1937, she took her vows. At that time, she chose the name Teresa because of St. Thérèse of Lisieux. St. Teresa described the calling to do missionary work was to "go out and give the life of Christ to the people."

In 1944, St. Teresa became principal at St. Mary's school. Two years later, she contracted tuberculosis and was no longer able to teach. On September 10, 1946, St. Teresa was traveling to a little-known town in the Himalayas known as Darjeeling to recover from the disease. On the train ride there, she received a "call within the call." She referred to this new call as follows: "And when that happens the only thing to do is to say yes. The message was quite clear that I was to give up all and follow Jesus into the slums to serve Him in the poorest of the poor. I knew it was His will and that I had to follow Him. There was no doubt that it was to be His work. I was to leave the convent and work with the poor, living among them. It was an order. I knew where I belonged, but I did not know how to get there."

St. Teresa was called by Jesus to establish a new religious community called the Missionaries of Charity. This order was started in 1950 and was dedicated to the poorest of the poor. She was a spiritual entrepreneur. The order has a constitution which states in part, "Our aim is to quench the infinite thirst of Jesus Christ on the Cross for love of souls. We serve Jesus in the poor, we nurse Him, feed Him, clothe Him, visit Him." In all the chapels of her order throughout the world, the words "I thirst" are written above the crucifixes there.

St. Teresa describes the proper measure of giving to others as giving until it hurts. She said, "We must grow in love, and to do this we must go on loving and loving and giving and giving until it hurts the way Jesus did. Do ordinary things with extraordinary love: little things like caring for the sick and the homeless, the lonely and the unwanted, washing and cleaning for them. You must give what will cost you something."

Our Blessed Mother Mary was a great role model for St. Teresa. Our Lady demonstrated tremendous purity, surrender, holiness, and spiritual motherhood. All the Missionaries of Charity pray to the Mother of Jesus fervently. St. Teresa prayed to our Blessed Mother Mary this way: "Mary, Mother of Jesus, give me your heart, so beautiful, so pure, so immaculate, so full of love and humility that I may be able to receive Jesus in the Bread of Life, love Him as you loved Him, and serve Him in the distressing disguise of the Poorest of the Poor."

Happiness and peace were a big part of the life of St. Teresa. She said, "We have a right to be happy and peaceful. We have been created for this, we are born to be happy, and we can only find true happiness and peace when we are in love with God: there is joy in loving God, great happiness in loving Him."

St. Teresa died on September 5, 1997. She was canonized on September 4, 2016, by Pope Francis. She is the patron saint of World Youth Day.

Lucinda Valley, *Mother Teresa: A Simple Path* (New York: Random House, 1995), XXI, XXII, XXV, XXX, 99, 179.

Life of St. Padre Pio

St. Padre Pio was born Francesco Forgione on May 25, 1887, in Pietrelcina, Italy, a small country town in southern Italy. He was one of seven children. His mother was Maria Giuseppa Di Nunzio Forgione, and his father was Grazio Mario Forgione. They were a very religious family, as they attended Mass and prayed the Rosary daily. They were devoted to Our Lady of Mount Carmel.

At five years of age, St. Padre Pio was already focused on his faith as he consecrated himself to Jesus. When he was ten years old, he told his parents that he wanted to be a friar. At age fifteen, he entered the Capuchin Friary of Morcone, Benevento. He took the habit and the name Br. Pio in honor of Pope St. Pius V. He celebrated his first Mass at the church of Our Lady of the Angels.

St. Padre Pio was given the wounds of Christ, the stigmata, when Jesus and Mary appeared to him on September 7, 1910. He experienced the invisible stigmata almost weekly for a few years in the form of the crowning with thorns. In 1916, he was assigned to the friary of San Giovanni Rotondo, which was located in the Gargano Mountains. He remained in this community for the rest of his life other than for brief periods of time. In 1918, St. Padre Pio had a vision of Jesus and was given the visible stigmata in his hands, feet, and side.

After receiving the visible stigmata, St. Padre Pio seldom left the friary. Soon, large numbers of people began to visit him. He heard confessions many hours each day. Many of these people said that he knew the details of their souls that were never discussed with him. Also, he spent time daily blessing the sick. A number of people said they were cured through the intercession of this saint.

When St. Padre Pio was a boy, his guardian angel appeared to him and became his companion for life. On one occasion, the saint told his confessor about his guardian angel. To test Padre Pio about his special friend, the confessor wrote Padre Pio a letter in Greek and asked him to translate it. This was a language that the saint did not know. Padre Pio returned the letter to the confessor translated from Greek to English. The confessor asked him how he was able to do it, and his response was that his guardian angel helped him.

Later, the saint wrote using foreign languages even though he never studied them. His knowledge came from his guardian angel. This very special saint often wrote letters to friends, encouraging them to recognize that their guardian angels were always with them.

St. Padre Pio died on September 23, 1968. Almost one hundred thousand people attended his funeral. He was canonized a saint on June 16, 2002, by Pope St. John Paul II. More than three hundred thousand people attended the ceremony in St. Peter's Square. Pope St. John Paul II described this saint as a witness to suffering, which can lead to a privileged path of sanctity.[44]

The saint wrote a prayer known as "Stay with Me, Lord." Some of the parts of his prayer are: "Stay with me, Lord, for it is

---

[44] Fr. Alessio Parente, O.F.M., *Send Me Your Guardian Angel*, 3rd ed. (Amsterdam, NY: Noteworthy Company, 1984).

necessary to have You present so that I do not forget You. You know how easily I abandon You. Stay with me, Lord, because I am weak and I need Your strength, that I may not fall so often. Stay with me, Lord, for You are my life, and without You, I am without meaning and hope. Stay with me, Lord, to show me Your will. Stay with me, Lord, so that I can hear Your voice and follow You.... Grant that I may love You with all my heart while on earth, so that I can continue to love You perfectly throughout all eternity, dear Jesus, Amen!"

About the Author

Richard Eason has been a permanent deacon in the Archdiocese of New Orleans since 2012 and is assigned to Good Shepherd Parish. He participates in several Catholic apostolates, including being on the board of directors of the Ozanam Inn homeless shelter and volunteering at St. Jude Nursing Home in New Orleans, and he serves in the community as a member of the ForeKids! Foundation. He is also a frequent speaker on Spiritual Excellence (as a series and study group) in Catholic parishes and prayer groups.

Deacon Richard graduated with honors from Tulane University with a degree in economics and from Loyola University New Orleans School of Law. He practices as a civil litigator with the regional law firm of Adams and Reese, LLC. He has served on the firm's executive committee and as a practice group leader for the litigation team. He has extensive trial experience in complex commercial and personal injury cases in state and U.S. district courts in Louisiana, Texas, and Mississippi. He has appeared before the U.S. 5th and 11th circuit courts of appeal and the U.S. Supreme Court.

Deacon Eason is blessed to be married to his wife, Rosalyn, and to have three sons, Blake, Kyle, and Grant; a daughter-in-law, Ashley; and two wonderful grandchildren, Evan and Clare.